Endorsements

Okoth's book deftly evaluates bystander involvement from every possible angle and explores the needs and motivations of citizen involvement through both a philosophical and pragmatic lens. Moving throughout the book, one gets a sense of citizen involvement in a global perspective that is unique to his work. In *Responding to Black Swans: Why Ordinary Citizens Matter,* there is a definite sense that citizens do, in fact, matter and that their involvement is a highly overlooked component of preparing for disaster at all levels. The book is easily read and understood and moves from the theoretical to the applied nature of citizen involvement swiftly and confidently. There is much to be learned from the widespread examples of citizen involvement Okoth explores. The book is a must-read for emergency planners, policymakers, and Good Samaritans alike.
—Angelica Bega Hart, Virginia Commonwealth University

Finally, a book that examines and justifies what happens on the ground. Bystanders can indeed play a greater role in emergency rescue efforts if provided with the basic skills. I highly recommend this book to everyone.
—Bani Orwa, PhD, Stirling International

Responding to Black Swans

WHY ORDINARY CITIZENS MATTER

Simon H. Okoth

WESTBOW
PRESS®
A DIVISION OF THOMAS NELSON
& ZONDERVAN

This book is a work of non-fiction. Unless otherwise noted, the author and the publisher make no explicit guarantees as to the accuracy of the information contained in this book and in some cases, names of people and places have been altered to protect their privacy.

Scriptures taken from the Holy Bible, New International Version®, NIV®. Copyright © 1973, 1978, 1984, 2011 by Biblica, Inc.™ Used by permission of Zondervan. All rights reserved worldwide. www.zondervan.com The "NIV" and "New International Version" are trademarks registered in the United States Patent and Trademark Office by Biblica, Inc.™

WestBow Press books may be ordered through booksellers or by contacting:

WestBow Press
A Division of Thomas Nelson & Zondervan
1663 Liberty Drive
Bloomington, IN 47403
www.westbowpress.com
1 (866) 928-1240

Because of the dynamic nature of the Internet, any web addresses or links contained in this book may have changed since publication and may no longer be valid. The views expressed in this work are solely those of the author and do not necessarily reflect the views of the publisher, and the publisher hereby disclaims any responsibility for them.

Any people depicted in stock imagery provided by Thinkstock are models, and such images are being used for illustrative purposes only. Certain stock imagery © Thinkstock.

ISBN: 978-1-5127-8724-5 (sc)
ISBN: 978-1-5127-8725-2 (hc)
ISBN: 978-1-5127-8723-8 (e)

Library of Congress Control Number: 2017907689

Print information available on the last page.

WestBow Press rev. date: 06/02/2017

To my children, Amy, Jona, and Jesse; grandchildren, Mazen Alexander, Ellie Josephine, and Kito Valentino; and loving wife, Elizabeth.

Contents

Acknowledgments

A number of people contributed to the final product of this book. First, I am grateful to Angelica Bega of the Wilder School of Government and Public Affairs at Virginia Commonwealth University for meticulously proofreading the manuscript. To graduate teaching assistants Brittany Keegan, a PhD student, and Bradley Corallo in the MPA program, both of Virginia Commonwealth University, for their initial edits, I am also thankful. I also appreciate Jesse Okoth (Traybien) with whom I debated this subject from time to time. His thoughtful questions triggered deeper thoughts both below and above the surface. To my daughter, Amy, who occasionally called me in the evenings from work to ask about my progress and insisted that I read over the phone what I wrote that day; her insights helped improve the arguments. I appreciate the comments by and understanding of the "First Lady" Elizabeth. Her challenge to my assumptions often led to additional research and introspection. Thanks to my students at Zayed University in Abu Dhabi and Virginia Commonwealth University who shared their views on related issues. I am equally indebted to all those who participated in the survey I conducted in Abu Dhabi, Maryland, West Virginia, Virginia, and Kenya. The data collected helped answer some of the intricate questions debated in selected chapters of this book. The publishing staff that rectified the somewhat messy draft into a readable format, you deserve the biggest of kudos.

Preface

One Easter weekend in 2000, my wife, Elizabeth, my brother James, his daughter Hilda, and I were driving from Nairobi, Kenya, to the western city of Kisumu, a journey of about five hours. Upon completing the drive across the floors of the Great Rift Valley and beginning to take the descent through a rather winding road from the tea plantation neighborhood of Kericho town, a private vehicle overtook us at a high speed. Before long, I noticed the same vehicle in a standstill position behind a truck parked on the opposite side of the road. I immediately alerted my passengers and slammed on the brakes. We got out and ran to the car because the vehicle appeared to have been involved in an accident. After forcing the doors open, we noticed that the driver had passed on, as his head lay motionless on the steering wheel. We left him intact and decided to remove the passenger from the front seat and laid him on the ground. Next we carried three female victims, who were still alive, from the floor of the backseat and laid them out next to the other victim. My wife waved down private vehicles heading in different directions in order to seek help. Fortunately, with the kind response of motorists, the ladies were rushed to Kericho District Hospital, some twenty minutes away, and the surviving man to Aga Khan Hospital in Kisumu, another ninety minutes away to the west. After we had reached our destination, the following day we decided to check on the condition of the victim at the Aga Khan Hospital, only to learn that he had passed on before arrival. As we later came to learn, the ladies had recovered at a Nairobi hospital. We were fortunate to meet two of them by their hospital beds later that month.

Almost two years later, my wife and I were driving from Western Kenya back to Nairobi where we lived. Hardly ten minutes' drive from Nakuru town, which is midway between Kisumu to the west and Nairobi to the center of Kenya, we noticed a passenger bus involved in a serious accident. Human bodies were strewn all over the field. Since it had just happened, when we reached the scene, some passengers appeared motionless and were probably dead, others were writhing in pain, and some seemed alive but maimed and simply staring. After parking our vehicle on the side of the road, we rushed to the scene and tried to assist in any way we could. Fortunately, several private vehicles had stopped to provide assistance to the victims. At the scene, we found one lady in pain, whom we brought to a Nakuru hospital. Upon arriving in Nairobi that evening with contact information of her next of kin, I managed to trace her husband and provided him with the details about the accident and of his wife's medical condition.

In 2010, my daughter, Amy, was involved in a car accident on her way from Baltimore to work a few miles outside of Washington, DC. A light truck ran a red light and rammed into her vehicle while she was waiting at the intersection. Within minutes, smoke engulfed her car as she struggled to get out. Passersby who witnessed the incident ran to her rescue and, on finding that she was able to speak, instructed her to stay put, as help would come soon. They were right. Someone who had seen the incident through an office window called 911, and within five minutes, a police car, an ambulance, and a fire truck were at the scene. She was then rushed to a nearby hospital where she recovered from emotional shock. Note the difference: the passersby did not pull Amy out of the vehicle but told her to stay put, something we will revisit later in this book.

I have heard of similar stories from people I have met. Strangely, four years into my college teaching in Virginia (United States), Kabul (Afghanistan), Riyadh (Saudi Arabia), and Abu Dhabi (United Arab Emirates), several newspaper and televised reports about ordinary people assisting victims of catastrophic events began to attract my attention. Consequently, I asked myself: what leads ordinary people like me, regardless of their locations across the world, to instinctively jump to assist others in distressful and harmful situations? I began to argue in my mind that there must be something intrinsic that unites us, we humans, to respond to emergencies that are potentially harmful to others. When I posed the same question to my family at a dinner table to see what they thought drove humans to assist others in danger, the unanimous response was, "a natural feeling," but I wanted to know more. Subsequently, I decided to conduct a systematic investigation as to why this is so. That is the genesis of this book.

The central thesis of this book is that unpredictable disasters ("black swans") are happening on an unprecedented scale, that ordinary citizens often are the first to help ("potent instinct"), and that official preparations and responses have been dangerously inadequate. How can governments better prepare for emergencies knowing these facts? The partial answer to this big question lies in the incorporation of ordinary citizens in emergency preparedness as the likely first responders. Another related question to which this book explores some answers is, how can the same instinct that drives ordinary people into assisting in emergency situations drive movements for broader political change in response to tragedy? These questions can be collapsed into three and framed as follows.

1. What motivates ordinary citizens to (or to want to) assist others in danger even when their own lives might be at stake? I hypothesize that potent instinct (PI) drives ordinary citizens to assist those in danger.

2. To what extent do human emotions (or PI) influence public policy and administrative decisions on how to mitigate, prepare for, and respond to catastrophic events? I hypothesize that human emotions have the tendency to influence political and administrative decisions about how and when to prepare and respond to catastrophic events.

3. How can governments better prepare for emergencies knowing these facts?
    It is my hypothesis that, given the tendency of emergencies to overwhelm the administrative capacity to respond effectively

and on time, agencies will improve their effectiveness by incorporating ordinary citizens into emergency plans, creating supportive structures and equipping them with basic skills and tools."

Central to this book is the number of cases gathered from different parts of the world that show how human instincts or emotions can drive ordinary people not trained in rescue operations to assist those in distress or danger. These narratives collected from newspaper reports and published materials, as well as from analyzed data of a survey conducted in 2012, seek to show that humans are naturally inclined to rescue others in danger not for some intrinsic or extrinsic reward but because "it is the right thing to do." It is the power of what I call the potent instinct (PI). This is the natural force in humans that urges an altruistic reaction to assist those in danger.

Although social research, particularly in psychology, is inconclusive about what drives humans to help others even when their own lives might be at stake, narrative evidence across nations supports the view that it is the instinct that stimulates our altruistic behavior and consequently causes a sympathetic response to those in distress. There are, however, some exceptions, such as the 1964 murder of Kitty Genovese, who was stabbed repeatedly on a street in Brooklyn, New York, while witnesses ignored her cries for help. It took more than forty-five minutes for a neighbor to finally call the police. In another example, a woman was gang-raped in India in December 2012. She was left writhing in pain by the roadside while screaming for help, but no one stopped to assist.

Although the reluctance to help those in life-threatening situations might invariably be explained by the circumstances, cultural norms, existing local laws, or by the nature of the situation, two schools of thought have debated this rare side of human behavior. One school of thought argues that the reluctance to provide assistance is most common in larger cities where witnesses think there is a greater chance that someone else will help. The second school of thought states that the opposite seems to be true. In smaller and less populated towns, passersby will most likely respond to the needs of a victim without much hesitation. This book focuses on the more common response, the instinct of those near an incident to rescue others in life-threatening situations, whether in bigger cities or smaller ones, rural villages or market towns. The bystanders are the true first responders, before professional rescuers arrive on the scene because we typically associate firemen, police, paramedics, and so on as first responders.

Although the term "emergency response" in its wider sense means putting preparation plans into action, as well as damage assessment, search and rescue, and even sheltering victims, this book uses the term specifically to denote actions taken by a bystander (not trained in rescue operations) to save lives and to prevent further injuries sustained by victims of an emergency.

The book is organized as follows: chapter 1 begins by examining some theoretical explanations as to why humans are driven to assist others in life-threatening situations.

Chapter 2 takes chapter 1 further by examining the unique characteristics of humans that make them act altruistically toward other beings, including those in emergency situations. Questions addressed are: What is human nature? What is humanness? What makes us special? Are we conditioned or innately endowed with some unique universal attributes that explain why the majority of us will exhibit emotion, empathy, and altruism toward strangers who face life-threatening situations? These are difficult but necessary questions worth exploring in order to appreciate our reactions toward emergencies.

Chapter 3 narrates a number of incidents in which ordinary bystanders have assisted those in an emergency. The chapter starts with a bomb blast that occurred in Nairobi, Kenya, in 1998. In that incident, exacted by Al-Qaeda operatives, 228 US embassy employees, as well as ordinary citizens who were in the vicinity at that time, perished. I examine, through content analysis of newspaper reports and other publications, how ordinary citizens moved in to rescue the victims by removing the rubble with their bare hands before professionals arrived. Even after the professionals took over the rescue operations, many untrained volunteers milled the scene of the incident on daily basis to extend help. Other cases from around the world are recounted to demonstrate this unique call to duty by ordinary citizens, even when their own lives might be in danger.

Thus, chapter 4 reports an empirical investigation of the question: What motivates ordinary citizens to want to rescue others in danger even when it is not safe to do so? The report validates the hypothesis that humans are naturally inclined to assist in emergencies and will voluntarily do so without expecting any form of reward.

Chapter 5 explores how human emotions (potent instinct) influence the timing of public policy and administrative decisions to put in place institutions/structures and laws (or plans) to mitigate, prepare for, and respond to catastrophic events. Specific efforts by the broader international community, national levels, and local levels are documented.

Chapter 6 presents the case for governments to incorporate ordinary citizens into emergency plans, arguably because they tend to be the first responders given their proximity to such events whenever they occur. Moreover, bystanders do so willingly without expecting any form of remuneration. Thus, my view is that intervention by bystanders can be a cost-effective means to responding to emergencies in urban and local communities, particularly when these ordinary citizens are already equipped with basic lifesaving skills.

Chapter 7 provides recommendations for policy makers, administrative agencies, nonprofits, and citizens for how best to prepare for this first-responder reality and needs.

Finally, in the appendix, a Basic Emergency Preparedness Guide for different types of catastrophic events is provided for ease of reference.

The book is intended for a variety of readers. First, policy makers and government agency officials charged with designing and executing emergency plans. The Nairobi incident, along with others cited in the book, can provide useful lessons from which to learn about emergency preparedness and response. Second, academics who will find the idea of including ordinary citizens in emergency response teams a cause for theoretical discourse. To the researcher, it's a book that includes realistic and useful accounts. Third, to the ordinary citizens, who from time to time find themselves in emergency situations, this book confirms the power of that instinct to help those in distress and danger. You are not alone.

Additionally, the book is intended for all of us. It encourages everyone to desist from selective empathy in which we tend to choose whom to assist and not to assist. Rather, we should not limit our rescue to those in abrupt emergencies such as accidents but also to those on the verge of long-term emergencies, including the homeless, the unemployed, sexually abused women and children, refugees, and the marginalized.

Chapter 1

Citizens' Responses to Emergencies: Some Explanations

It is impossible for people to see other humans tremendously
mistreated [or suffer tragedies], and not do anything ... If
they view the victims as good human beings, bystanders will
experience empathy. As the victims suffer, so they suffer.
—Ervin Staub, 1989

Explanations as to why ordinary citizens not trained in emergency rescue respond to emergencies (or life-threatening situations) can be divided into two categories: theoretical and nontheoretical. Theories can be defined as sets of ideas that consistently explain why things happen or to justify a course of action. Good theories can also predict the occurrence of a phenomenon in some determined or undetermined future. Scientists from all walks of life rely on theories to find explanations for myriad events or even behaviors of Homo sapiens and other species across the universe. It is important to note, however, that theories are generally proven explanations that can consistently explain why something happens the way it does regardless of geographical or cultural differences.

Another way to explain an occurrence of something over time is

1

with hypothesis or proposition. I prefer to use the word *proposition* because this is what many laypeople use to explain why things happen—tentative answers, if you will. As readers will notice in the discussion of examples that follow, some of the propositions are credible but cannot be generalized across cultures or national boundaries. Propositions can be viewed as transient ideas that change with time. Even though theories also change, once better ones have been formulated and accepted, they often tend to be permanent.

In what follows, some theories and propositions are examined in terms of how they attempt to explain what makes us—humans—assist others in danger, even when we don't know them or even when such actions may expose the rescuer to greater risk. Because the boundaries between theories and propositions can be imprecise at times, I treat the following explanations under one rubric: "Some Explanations."

Some Explanations

Sociologists begin their explanations by looking at the way communities are structured. These include belief systems, norms and values, family ties, friendships, power relationships, and groups (formal and informal) (Quarantelli, 1978; Forrest, 1978). These structures work as mechanisms for solving problems, which in turn means communities can be viewed as problem-solving entities within any given society. Quarantelli adds that values are an important component because they help communities determine what is good and what is bad. Therefore, to help others in danger is deemed in a number of societies as a good thing. As it were, we ought to be our brother and sister's keeper.

Belief systems can often be a good indicator of why people in a particular community or culture behave in certain ways or do certain things that are considered somewhat different from those in other cultures, particularly in relation to the requirements of some natural forces. Therefore, to rescue or not to rescue a known burglar or sex offender and his family from a burning house can be evaluated through this lens of a belief system. Another factor that determines the responsiveness to a life-threatening event is the extent to which the community is experienced with such events and the quality of previous responses. This is important because people have the tendency to evaluate how they have previously performed on a specific task and then use this information to determine how to best respond or act the next time. Additionally, individuals are more likely to respond to emergencies when they have prior relevant training and knowledge (Forrest, 1978).

Another common explanation is that of social cohesion among groups. It has been opined that humans will gravitate toward social cohesion whenever an incident that affects their communal well-being emerges abruptly. As Solnit (2009, p. 489) has observed, "[When] faced with a common trauma, individuals put aside their social differences in order to provide material and emotional support to victims." A good example was the manner in which a number of ordinary people who happened to be close to the attack on the World Trade Center in New York on September 11, 2001, quickly grouped to assist with the initial rescue operation.

In a study to investigate why a number of German bystanders joined in the destructive acts that resulted in the mass killings of the Jews, Ervin Staub (1989, p. 49) discovered that "bystanders can exert tremendous influence on other bystanders." Thus, if a group is seen beating a victim for a reason not clearly known to the bystander, it is likely that the latter will join in simply because the person being beaten is perceived as bad or as someone who must have done something not acceptable to a particular family, organization, or society.

In another example, when one is hit by a car and a bystander runs to assist the victim, other bystanders will be drawn into the scene to provide assistance as well. As Staub (1978, p. 49) found in a separate study:

> When in an emergency people remain passive, do nothing, ... express no concern on hearing distress sounds or seeing smoke filling a room, when by what they say or by their inaction define the situation as one in which no action is needed, they greatly reduce the likelihood that other bystanders take action or attempt to help. When they define a situation as one in which help is needed, or tell another person to help, they increase helping.

This observation suggests that action or inaction by one or more people in an emergency situation is to a large extent determined by bystander influence on another bystander. As in the case of Kitty Genovese, who cried for help as she suffered stabbings by an attacker at night in New York, no one helped despite the fact that a number of people saw the incident through their windows. I revisit this case in chapter 2.

According to Staub's hypothesis, had one person volunteered to assist, it is likely that others would have done so as well. As in the case of the Indian female student who was gang-raped and left writhing in pain on a street, it is strange that in the populated streets nobody stopped to help. While the local culture, norms, and practices may have explained why there was no action by bystanders, Staub's study suggests that the inaction was because others did nothing as well. Therefore, observing actions—good or bad—by other bystanders tends to explain responses to incidents that are either abrupt or systemic (e.g., mass killings of Jews by the Nazis of Germany). The interactions among bystanders to assess whether to assist or not assist can also explain what motivates bystanders to get involved in emergency situations. This view is supported by several other studies, including that of Latane and Darley (1970). Their study reached the same conclusion but added that there is diffusion of responsibility among the likely helpers that results from social influence.

The idea of first making a judgment to either assist or not to assist brings up another familiar concept: rationality. Humans have, in my view, pedantically accorded themselves the label "rational" and often pride themselves as the only animal species that possesses the ability to make decisions after weighing the pros and cons. In the case of an emergency, it can be assumed that a human being will ask the following question before trying to get involved with a rescue (unless he or she is a rescue professional): is saving a victim's life beneficial to society compared to the costs of my effort to give her a new lease on life?

We tend to believe that this cognitive exercise is arguably part of human nature. Theoretically, this is how this process works. Whenever one is faced with a decision to make, no matter how rushed it may seem, she will presumably determine first the degree of urgency or importance of doing something about it. She will then weigh the benefits that will accrue and the costs of taking action. Finally, she will decide whether to go with an action or no action, guided by whether the potential benefits of the action outweigh the costs of intervention. This means that if costs are deemed too high compared to the projected benefits, then the rational thing to do is not to take an action. This perspective provides us with an interesting way of analyzing the decision by ordinary citizens to either intervene or not to intervene in emergencies that occur in close proximity to where they are at that moment.

Let us take a hypothetical case to illustrate the logic of rational decision making when it comes to real emergencies. The point I want to drive forward is whether bystanders do in fact engage in the rational process before deciding to rescue an individual facing a life-threatening situation.

Imagine for a moment that you are driving along a country road or in a residential neighborhood where the legal posted speed limit is twenty-five miles per hour. Just ahead, you notice a hit-and-run accident in which a fast-moving vehicle has hit a young woman who was cycling across the road. The victim is tossed to the side of the road and poses no danger to other vehicles on the road, including yours. You instantaneously decide to pull over and run to the victim. You stand by her and make a call to an emergency line—in the United States to 911. You then run back to your car to get a slow-down/yield road sign to warn other approaching vehicles about the emergency. As a result of your quick action, ambulatory service crew and firefighters are at the scene hardly five minutes from the time you called. The victim is rushed to the hospital and declared out of danger after several hours of observation and treatment. The questions are these: Did you cognitively employ each of the rational processes to take the actions? Did you pull up by the roadside, run to the victim, call 911, and get the slow-down road sign from your car? Or was it an instinctive response that had nothing to do with that rational process? It is a general experience to some of us that in times of emergency, our decisions are "bounded rational." That is, we assess only a few of the variables without necessarily going into the details of rational assessment of costs and benefits. Instead, we are guided by what is "good enough" (or satisfactory) in a given situation. I find the latter to be more relevant in situations of emergency.

While a take on this will certainly vary depending on where one sits or stands, I recently posed the same question to a number of friends and relatives to get their perspectives. Traybien, a twenty-seven-year-old filmmaker and photographer based in Richmond, Virginia, argued that whenever a bystander witnesses an emergency, he or she will instinctively jump in, in an attempt to rescue the victim. If one has to first go through a mental process of weighing the degree of seriousness of the incident, evaluating the potential benefits and costs of saving the victim, and then deciding what action to take, then the best thing is not to do anything at all. In the real world, there is a tendency to act based on gut feelings—and this takes a matter of seconds, not minutes. Traybien probably has a point here. In practice, rational decision making tends to take a bit of time and thus can easily reduce our ability to save lives. Reflect back for a second about the neighbors who apparently assessed the conditions outside of their apartments when Kitty Genovese cried for help in the wee hours of the night after being attacked by a man who stabbed her repeatedly at different intervals. The first neighbor switched on his lights after hearing the scream and then went back to sleep. He later rose up, probably after rationally processing what to do, and then shouted through his window, "Leave her alone." Yes, the attacker did, albeit briefly. As Genovese dragged herself closer to the door of her apartment, the attacker returned and stabbed her again, leaving her for dead. Again, it was at the forty-fifth to fiftieth minute that one of the neighbors, probably the same man who yelled at the victim earlier, called the police emergency line. Genovese was taking her last breath as the police arrived, and she died on the way to the hospital.

The exercise of rationality in the case of an emergency, especially at night, brings up a different perspective suggested by my spouse, Elizabeth. In response to the role of rationality, she says the analytical concept for understanding rational action is, "Why?" Generally, the employment of a rational process at any given time is guided by an attempt to respond to why I should do something about a problem or incident. Thus, finding answers to such a question calls into play the rational process. In a real emergency that one has just witnessed, there is no time to rationalize. The primary thought that goes through one's mind is, *I need to help, now.* At that time, Elizabeth contends, there is no time to ask why one must give help or not. In her own experience, most people who have witnessed an incident will first assess the situation and then make the decision to stop or not stop. This situation changes particularly at night when the likelihood that someone will stop is remote. At that time, Elizabeth contends, there is no time to ask why one must give help or not.

Another important and interesting explanation is the timing of the response to an emergency. Schwartz and Gottlieb (1980) argued that the choice made by individuals to intervene or not to intervene in an emergency near them is determined by two factors: the seriousness of the incident and the appropriateness of their intervention. Although it takes only a few seconds or even minutes to choose action or inaction, the bystander will first observe and assess the seriousness of the incident. If the incident is viewed as less life-threatening, then the bystander will likely not intervene. However, if the situation is assessed as grave, the bystander will be more likely to quickly and instinctively move into action. Consider a hypothetical situation to illustrate this point.

You are in a strange city vacationing, and you are sitting by a swimming pool. You see a child about two years old on the side of the pool, attempting to get into the ten-feet-deep water. You are not even sure who the parents are. You look again, and the child slips into the water. You instinctively jump out of the comfort of your seat, and within seconds you are in that pool with your clothes on trying to save the child. Another person follows you into the water, and together you bring the child out alive. She is completely oblivious to what is going on. The mother comes after a few minutes, screaming and wondering what happened, and thanks you both with tears rolling down her face. Was the timing of your action influenced by the potential seriousness of the incident? Were your action and that of the other person appropriate? Did you feel like it was an obligation to act? Why? Was it the right thing to do? If your answer is yes to the latter, you could be part of the 80 percent of ordinary people who successfully respond to community emergencies, according to the latest research findings (Phoenix Homeland Defense Bureau, 2011).

Studies conducted by McDonald, Charlesworth, and Graham (2015) to determine factors leading to action or inaction by bystanders provide answers to some of the questions posed in the above hypothetical case. In their study to understand why people intervened in cases of sexual abuse in Australian workplace, the scholars found that there were three compelling factors (p. 4).

1. *The situation*: is the incident certain or ambiguous, and what is its moral intensity?
2. *Moral responsibility belief*: is it one's moral responsibility to act or not to act?
3. *Costs and benefits of action*: Is the action meant to redress injustice (or provide relief from serious injuries)? Do the benefits of intervention outweigh the costs?

Any intervention by bystanders in sexual harassment situations were primarily influenced by the level of certainty that the incident is real, the feeling that is a responsibility of the witness to do something, and whether such intervention will provide relief to the victim. The latter view of weighing the costs and benefits before assisting in an emergency is consistent with Hoffman's reciprocal altruism perspective (1981, p. 125) that suggests that we are more likely to assist those in danger once we figure out that the likely cost of doing so is less than what we might expect to gain by the act. Under this assumption, the helper envisions herself in the same position as the victim and therefore extends the act because it is a low-risk game. In other words, it is cost-effective for a bystander to assist a victim. The victim gains, and I lose nothing by giving the help.

A related theoretical explanation is addressed by Martin Hoffman (1981) in an article titled "Is altruism part of human nature?" Hoffman raises the following important questions: Are our actions to save others from life-threatening situations God-given? Are we naturally wired to do good to those in distress? He uses Darwin's theory of natural selection to argue that only the strongest members of a species shall survive. This evolutionary biological perspective, therefore, suggests that humans must compete with each other to survive and hence it is unlikely that they will find it rational to help others in need. He alternatively evokes the canons of psychology that support egoistic motivation to assist others from dangerous situations—altruism.

According to *Oxford English Dictionary*, altruism is "selfless concern for the well-being of others." *Webster's Dictionary* defines it as "feelings and behavior that show a desire to help other people and a lack of selflessness." Such actions, including actions taken by organizations or even nations, can be seen through humanitarian and emergency aid, the donation of a kidney to a dying child, surrogate motherhood, or the rescue of Jews threatened by mass killings under Nazi Germany. It is also important to distinguish between altruism and empathy, as both terms can be confusing.

Empathy, as defined by *Oxford English Dictionary*, is "the ability to understand and appreciate another person's feelings, experience, etc." *Webster's Dictionary* defines it as "the action of understanding, being aware of, being sensitive to, and vicariously experiencing the feelings, thoughts, and experience of another of either the past or present without having the feelings, thoughts, and experience fully communicated in an objectively explicit manner." In other words, it is a distanced response to someone's condition (Hoffman, 1981). This distinction, however, does not suggest that the two terms are not related. As Hoffman has convincingly argued, the arousal of empathy can lead to altruistic behavior in most of us. Empathy can be detected in individuals through their bodily expressions or verbal statements that can imply they care and would be willing to help if an opportunity presents itself. A study by Sagi and Hoffman (1976) reveals that a one- to two-day-old baby will respond to the sound of another baby's cry by crying as well. This is a sign of empathy to someone else in distress. If altruism is a consequence of empathy, then it can be argued that the desire to assist members of our species facing danger is part of human nature. I, therefore, tend to believe that we humans, for the most part, empathize although we may not be able to actually assist due to circumstances or any other inhibiting factors, such as distance or limited resources.

Let's get back to altruism as a force that explains our impulse to assist those in emergencies. I recount selected theoretical explanations by Hoffman because of their aptness to understanding the thesis of this book and to the questions raised in the preface. First is the Group Selection Perspective (p. 122–3). This perspective takes us back in history to humans as hunters and gatherers. History shows that from the very beginning of time, Homo sapiens grouped together as social animals and to ensure survival by working together to compete against other species. Therefore, the survival of its own group has factored into our general behavior as families, communities, or nation-states wherein we project our defense and protection. This is probably why a stranger would sound a warning of an oncoming danger about to harm someone else she doesn't even know. It is, so to speak, an impulse to defend our cooperative existence.

The second perspective is kin selection (Hoffman, 1975). This is the argument that our propensity to assist others is enhanced by our relatedness to them through kinship. Kinship is a "form of natural selection that favors altruistic behavior toward close relatives resulting in an increase in the altruistic individual's genetic contribution to the next generation" (Dictionary.com). From this premise, it can be assumed that we humans will be driven to save our close kith and kin involved in an emergency because of the innate desire to ensure the survival of our genes into the next generation. The same argument can be extended to relationships by tribe, race, religion, organization, or citizenship (Eberhard in Hoffman, 1975).

The third perspective is egoistic motivational arousal factor (p. 125–126). The premise of this perspective is that humans are innately selfish and therefore will likely assist others in danger merely to seek social approval and self-reward. In the first case, individuals will want to show empathy or altruism because they lack self-esteem and are generally deemed antisocial by peers. By helping, the argument goes, they expect to be brought back to the fold by the other members of their group (age mates, classmates, gender, tribe, etc.). The counterargument to this position is that such individuals will assist only after ensuring witnesses are around before they jump into the helping action. Ordinarily, helping those in life-threatening situations tends to occur abruptly, and therefore those who assist don't generally wait to see if others are around to witness their act.

The second scenario of this egoistic perspective is even more interesting. It hypothesizes that our helping in emergencies is driven by the desire to "avoid anxiety or guilt, or to conform to an internalized idea" (Hoffman, p. 134). Although scientific evidence of this position is scanty, there are some people who would want to assist simply to avoid being counted as inhumane. For example, Hoffman adds, they may vote yes to a legislation to provide public housing to the homeless even though they believe that homelessness is due to indolence, people who are not ready to work hard in a free market economy. In this case, the legislator is trying to conform and to avoid guilt.

As many of us are probably aware, the impulse to assist others in distress can also be taught in schools, by families, or by cultures. Moreover, it can be acquired through experiential learning or conditioning. Similarly, the desire to assist those in danger can be influenced by cultural practices, religious teachings, or state laws. Of particular interest are emergency-related state laws practiced in several parts of the United States. A good example is the Good Samaritan law. For those not familiar with the concept of "Samaritan," let me take you back to the Christian holy text, the Bible. The New Testament, as it is officially referred, is an account of the teachings of Jesus Christ. Therein, according to the Gospel of St. Luke, chapter 10:25–37, Jesus offered the now famous parable of the Good Samaritan, and it reads as follows:

> On one occasion an expert in the law stood up to test Jesus. "Teacher," he asked, "what must I do to inherit eternal life?"
>
> "What is written in the Law?" he replied. "How do you read it?"
>
> He answered, "'Love the Lord your God with all your heart and with all your soul and with all your strength and with all your mind'; and, 'Love your neighbor as yourself.'"
>
> "You have answered correctly," Jesus replied. "Do this and you will live."

But he wanted to justify himself, so he asked Jesus, "And who is my neighbor?"

In reply, Jesus said: "A man was going down from Jerusalem to Jericho when he was attacked by robbers. They stripped him of his clothes, beat him and went away, leaving him half dead. A priest happened to be going down the same road, and when he saw the man, he passed by on the other side. So too, a Levite, when he came to the place and saw him, passed by on the other side. But a Samaritan, as he traveled, came where the man was; and when he saw him, he took pity on him. He went to him and bandaged his wounds, pouring on oil and wine. Then he put the man on his own donkey, brought him to an inn and took care of him. The next day he took out two denarii and gave them to the innkeeper. 'Look after him,' he said, 'and when I return, I will reimburse you for any extra expense you may have.' "Which of these three do you think was a neighbor to the man who fell into the hands of robbers?"

The expert in the law replied, "The one who had mercy on him." Jesus told him, "Go and do likewise." (BibleGateway.com)

Given the Christian nation that it is, many US states have adopted what legally came to be known as Good Samaritan laws. A Good Samaritan (GS) is one who voluntarily offers help to someone desperate for immediate first aid or medical care. In practice, it applies to a person providing aid to a victim of an emergency, as many did in the aftermath of 9/11, Hurricane Katrina, which hit New Orleans in 2005, and Hurricane Sandy, which destroyed lives and property in the northeastern part of the United States in 2012. Many people around the globe will testify to this; we witness or see reports of heroes who save the lives of heart attack victims, of choking children, and much more. Some of the readers of this book have been Good Samaritans at least one or more times. Examples of Good Samaritans in action are the subject of chapter 2.

Let me review briefly how the Good Samaritan law works in the United States. If I find a total stranger named Joe, for example, unconscious and not responding after being involved in an accident, and I decide to provide first aid, the aid should be generally rendered on the basis of implied approval by the victim. However, if Joe is conscious, I should first ask him if I can help, and then only provide aid if given permission. The reason is to avoid being liable for any further injuries should a claim be filed against me. A number of states have Good Samaritan laws to protect voluntary and humane acts. Two caveats to this law are important: the aid should only be provided at the scene of the incident, and a reward should not be the motivating factor for providing that aid. Therefore, the law does not protect an individual who volunteers to provide first aid purposely for self-reward in terms of financial compensation or otherwise.

Arguably, the United States is one of the most advanced nations in the world today with systems in place to respond to emergencies. But given the size of the country and the fact that emergency responders cannot be everywhere each second and hour, Good Samaritans (or bystanders, as they are called in this book) near an incident often avail themselves to rescue those in danger. However, the institutionalization of Good Samaritan laws by a number of states can promote or limit the degree to which ordinary people not trained in emergency rescue will be willing to provide aid to those involved in accidents or in other life-threatening situations.

While the above explanations tend to find their basis in formal studies, it is worth considering laypersons' explanations. I recite two of them here simply to show that such simplistic explanations, often based on norms and beliefs of a people, can just be as plausible as those offered by academics. I recently met an American with some medical background who explained that the reason why humans feel compassion for each other, especially when one is faced with a life-threatening situation, is because we are all connected to one another through a life-giving force, the blood. Consider for example a situation of blood donation.

Generally, when you donate blood and after it has been determined to be free of any contamination (or infection), it will be labeled according to its grouping. For example, O-, O+, B, B-, B+, AB, etcetera. No other demographic information, such as race (Indian American, white, black), age, or gender (male/female), is included on the label. Thereafter, it is stored in a blood bank according to types. Now, say a young Caucasian girl is bedridden after losing a great deal of blood in an unfortunate road accident; the bank will simply look for available blood of the same type as that of the patient. In this scenario, there is a certain degree of chance that the blood she receives might come from either an African American or a Latino. The good thing is, regardless of who donates that blood, the young girl has been given a new chance at life. As one trauma expert explains, this ability of human blood to sustain that of a stranger makes us believe that when another person is being harmed and there is reason to believe she is not at fault, we readily feel the urge to offer help.

Perhaps it is for this foregoing reason that the popular saying "Blood is thicker than water" was developed. Interestingly, I find some semblance of this explanation to the notion of "kin selection" hypothesis presented by Hoffman (1985). He suggests that our predisposition to assist strangers or relatives is heightened by our affiliation through genes—the impulse to save human genes or species from extinction. Many of us today will disagree with the indiscriminate killings or genocides that take place around the globe.

Another explanation shared by a female student of mine in Abu Dhabi, United Arab Emirates (UAE), comes from Islamic saying, *elnaz le elnaz,* which means "people are for people." According to Arabic culture, at least the one I encountered in the UAE, humans were created for other humans. This means the reason we are humans is to do something positive to other humans. Literally, it implies that I am my neighbor's keeper. If, for example, Africa's fiercest snake charges at a little girl, it is not most likely that you run away and leave the girl to fend for herself, but instead you would probably look for a way to rescue her. By extension, *elnaz le elnaz* connotes the altruistic side of humans. In humanistic terms, we have the moral and social obligation to assist those who are in some form of distress, such as sickness, accident, poverty, and refugee.

As I conclude this chapter, it is apparent that there are several reasons why humans have the urge to intervene whenever another fellow being faces a life-threatening situation. However, at the very foundation of that desire to intervene are humanitarian values: willingness, competence, the feeling of obligation, and personal courage (Axelsson, 2001).

Most of these are learned through socialization. As I have attempted to show throughout the rest of this book, however, most interventions are prompted by our innate instinct—something most people I have interacted with about this topic say is difficult to define. That is why the majority prefer such words as "feeling," "gut," "just did it," etcetera.

Chapter 2

What Makes Humans Unique

The motivation to help other people in distress is
linked to our [natural] ability to empathize with and
identify with (perhaps even love) other people.
—Lisa Mastain, 2006

Rightly or wrongly, humans have been thought of as possessing the
following traits: love, hatred, anger, aggression, sympathy, altruism,
communication, intelligence, and instinctiveness. Even if these traits
varied among individuals, we can safely say that they define who we
are as humans. The previous chapter reviewed a number of theoretical
explanations as to why people will respond to emergencies by trying
to rescue the victims involved. Those explanations, however, did not
examine what is unique about human nature and why they react this way.
One primary question I would like to address in this brief chapter is: are
we conditioned or innately endowed with some unique attributes that
make us exhibit emotions, empathy, and altruism toward strangers faced
by life-threatening situations? If this is true, then why do some people
fail to show empathy or altruism by not extending help to victims of
emergency even when they are in a position to do so? These are difficult

but necessary questions worth exploring in order to appreciate our reactions toward emergencies in general.

The debate over who we are in terms of human nature has lingered for centuries. Ancient Greek philosophers and contemporary scholars, including sociologists, have kept this debate alive without any convincing consensus. Consequently, a number of perspectives have been advanced in the literature, with each attempting to convince the reader to walk their line. I examine some of these viewpoints with the hope that we can arrive at some vague understanding about human nature and what is meant by "humanness." To put it differently, are there specific behaviors or moral laws that define humanness? What is it that we all can claim is indispensable in order to be considered human (Mitchel, 1972)? Answering these questions can potentially bring us closer to appreciating why, in a number of cases, the majority of humans will react in particular ways whenever emergencies occur.

Socrates was probably the first among the Greeks and Western philosophers to address the subject of human nature. In speaking about ethics, Socrates argued that an extremely good person is one who is honest, courageous, wise, and "truly concerned about the welfare of others" (Pojman, 2006, p. 32). These desired values resonate with biblical views of humans that portray us as godly, given that we were created in His image. It is no wonder that Plato described humans in spiritual and semi-divine terms. Socrates was, however, skeptical about human nature years before he was accused of heresy (i.e., rejecting Olympian gods). It is the evil he saw in humans that took him to the paths and hills of Athens, preaching to the youth about human virtues and goodness. Aristotle, who came after Plato, emphasized human character in terms of his role in society. He compared a human to a knife whose function is to cut, whereas a good knife is one that must cut better. Therefore, a virtuous person must be judged by his/her good actions that spring from the character (Pojman, 2006, p. 62).

Later philosophers, including Hobbes, Rousseau, Freud, Sartre, Locke, ethologists (i.e., those who study the human character and its formation) and sociologists alike, have similarly advanced some rather convincing, if not romantic, views of human nature (Midgley, 1995).

Hobbes, for example, thought of humans as bad, insensitive, and unsocial, while Rousseau took the opposite view; humans are humble, peaceful, and kind in nature. Jean-Paul Sartre and his contemporary existentialists were of the opinion that there is nothing like human nature. Instead, humans are defined by lifetime conditioning rather than some questionable attributes they are born with. This view mirrors that of sociologists who seem to believe that a human is defined by the environment in which she lives, including the dominant culture of her society. Hence, if I am afraid of heights, I cannot claim it to be innate but rather a result of societal conditioning that heights are a threat to human lives. That is, a small slip can result in suicidal death. The crux of these thoughts is that humans do not have instincts; their fears (or abrupt reactions) to threats are, by and large, conditioned by society. This takes us to the most important topic of this book, instincts.

Instinct and emotion are two important features that define human nature and make us unique from other species. Instinct can be described variously. *Webster's Dictionary* online defines it as "a largely inheritable and unalterable tendency of an organism to make a complex and specific response to environmental stimuli without involving reason." This definition is interesting because it raises a contentious statement: "without reason." It is indeed arguable when, in an emergency, a person jumps into action to save a victim from fire or from drowning. This instinctive reaction to danger, I would argue, is supported by reason because saving a victim is often triggered first by assessing whether the person will be harmed or not. If the degree of certainty is higher, then the bystander will do all she can to save the victim. This decision making, however short a time it takes, involves reasoning.

Ethologists (i.e., those who study animal behavior) maintain that we have instincts and that this attribute is something we are born with. This means that we are born to feel or act in some particular ways (Midgley, 1995, p. 19). It also implies that we can tell that my grandchild Ellie Josephine, born six months ago, will, for example, act on instincts in response to some external stimuli as she grows up. This view is supported by psychologists who admit that we have certain inclinations, such as friendship, grouping, crying, or even laughter, that are genetically fixed.

This is what Midgley (p. 53) calls "Closed Instincts", the opposite of which is "Open Instincts." The former suggests that we owe part of our instincts to nature and the latter to experience. For example, we humans have been thought to be naturally aggressive, judging by the frequency with which we engage in wars and methodically kill members of our own species. As controversial a stance as it may sound, it is true that a toddler does not exhibit this aggressive quality until later when the parents and the society in which she lives have taught her how to be aggressive toward enemies. This is the essence of Open Instinct.

Emotion is another natural trait that makes human beings unique. According to Dictionary.com, emotion is "any strong agitation of the feelings actuated by experiencing love, hate, fear, etc., and usually accompanied by certain physiological changes, as increased heartbeat or respiration, and often overt manifestation, as crying or shaking." Emotion is a spontaneous mental expression of feelings, such as hate, love, or even sorrow (Wilson 1972). Liah Greenfeld (Psychology.com) classifies human emotion into two categories: primary emotions and secondary emotions. The former is first experienced through sensations that are translated into direct reaction to things like pleasure, pain, fear, joy, and hunger. The purpose is to ensure an organism's survival. This type of emotion is, arguably, common to all human species and probably in most animals. The other, secondary emotions, is exhibited through a blend of sensations such as affection, pleasure, and relations between humans. It is this secondary emotion that pushes humans to express sorrow, compassion, or sense of disappointment whenever they lose someone they know and love. Hence, I contend that these two types of emotion are part and parcel of human nature and therefore not easy to control.

Another attribute that defines human nature is aggression. This can be defined as a "behavior that causes or leads to harm, damage or destruction of another organism" (Siegel and Victoroff, 2009, p. 210). A number of scholars and laymen contend that aggression is hardwired into our brains from birth and cannot be altered. This is often exhibited through expressions of anger (i.e., defensive rage) and what Siegel and Victoroff (p. 209) call "predatory attack." Defensive rage is generally triggered by either a perceived or real threat. Hence the need to defend the self or others from potential harm. If this is true, does it adequately explain why we tend to aggressively respond to life-threatening objects or actions of others (including animal species) that threatens our peace or lives?

The second type of aggression, predatory attack, is a conditioned response that is influenced by factors outside of the responder and therefore requires planning. Such external factors include education, indoctrination, religion, cultural norms and practices, and other social constructs of particular societies. That is why people in other cultures have the tendencies to react differently to social issues that are disturbing and threaten social order.

Prosocial behavior is conceived as one of the human traits. It can be described as deliberate conduct meant to benefit another person. Such kind of behavior includes collaborating, sharing, and helping (Hawley, 2014). It also concerned with the welfare of others, such as comforting and providing for immediate and long-term needs. This kind of behavior is of interest because it can help us understand why some of us assist others even when doing so can be costly in terms of time, energy, or risk to life. What is more interesting is the fact that people will engage in this helping behavior even when they do not derive any obvious personal benefit. Why then do they do it? Psychologists have offered a number of reasons: one, the behavior is something nurtured from childhood, especially by parents and society, and reinforced as good behavior. That is why I see my grandson Mazen encouraged to share his biscuit with other children.

Although unique to humans, the motivation behind such kind of behavior is both altruistic and egoistic. Some use their prosocial tendencies to benefit others, while some focus on benefiting solely the self. One question worth asking is: is prosocial behavior an inborn trait or something that we acquire through socialization?

Pity (or sympathy), some might argue, is related to prosocial behavior. Others will see it as an inborn trait. The aim of pity is to protect the vulnerable from suffering. In practice, many people will have pity on those who face life-threatening situations. Some will intervene and do something in favor of the suffering, while others may turn their heads away. We witness or read about these behaviors from time to time.

The ability to communicate verbally and in writing is also unique to humans. When we observe an event, there is a tendency to react in a certain way depending on communication cues we obtain from the incident. Our interpretation of the event will change when that occurrence is accompanied with more overt forms of communication. For example, in an emergency, a victim might cry in pain or shout for help. Because of our ability to hear and interpret the meaning of verbal cues, or expressions on the face, we will react either to assist or to turn the other way.

If, as has been shown above, humans bear some common traits, then why do some people not demonstrate these attributes in emergency situations whenever victims need help? We have heard of tales where vulnerable females cried for help from the hands of murderers and rapists, but bystanders simply passed by. What happens to the prosocial behavior we claim to possess? Or does the presence of others (or bystander effect) alter or diminish the efficacy of prosocial behavior? Does cultural conditioning have anything to do with it?

Regardless of the variation in which different people react to emergency situations, evidence in the next chapter convincingly shows that a majority of humans, regardless of their cultural and geographical contexts, react in a similar manner whenever they witness a life-threatening incident. For the most part, they demonstrate the attributes that seem to unite all human species: empathy, altruism, pity, prosocial behavior, and positive feeling toward someone facing a life-threatening situation. It is what many describe as "feeling" or "instinctive reaction."

Chapter 3

Potent Instinct at Work: Global Examples

Every human mind feels pleasure in doing good to another.
—Thomas Jefferson, third president of the United States of America

The Nairobi Bomb Blast

It was about 10:40 a.m. on Thursday, August 7, 1998. The day was as ordinary as any other in Nairobi, Kenya. People went about their business as usual. *Matatus* (minivan taxis) made their rounds in the city picking up and dropping off passengers along Haile Selassie, Kenyatta, Moi, and Harambee Avenues, among others. The weather was close to perfect, and inside the US embassy, the marines, along with American personnel and Foreign Service National employees (FSNs), continued with their daily routines. Some people walked in, others walked out of the embassy. And then, as if it were ordained to happen right on the button, a bomb went off. The blast repeated one more time, and within minutes, smoke and fire enveloped what seemed to be a totally ruptured piece of balloon. The five-floor embassy building had its southern wing shattered, although the northern half facing Moi Avenue remained intact except for the blown-off windows. It was surreal, total chaos.

Behind the embassy, a multistory Cooperative Bank House that contained banking halls and offices of Teachers Service Commission employees had its glass windows shattered, and the side café and bookstore facing the embassy ruptured, killing people. To the southwest of the embassy was a five-floor Ufundi Cooperative Building. That too went down with everyone in it. Further south, at the Central Bank of Kenya, about a hundred meters away, pieces of rock from the ceiling and shattered glass from the windows fell everywhere, forcing employees, including the spouse of this writer, to scamper for safety under the tables. In downtown Nairobi, it was total pandemonium as people ran in different directions for safety. No one knew where to go. It was as if an earthquake had occurred, causing total confusion. Fortunately, those who were briefly sane and had the hunch of what might have happened ran toward the American embassy where smoke was billowing furiously into the sky.

Immediately after the incident, along Haile Selassie Avenue, automobiles of different shapes were aflame with passengers inside. Pedestrians who happened to be passing by were either dead or writhing in pain with some parts of their bodies blown off or deeply cut. Others were found to have burned to death in parked vehicles. The print media quoted witnesses who described the grisly scene as follows:

> Passengers on a bus outside the embassy incinerated in their seats, of shattered cars smoldering in the street with passengers draped out the windows, of dazed and bleeding survivors lying on the ground pleading for help ... injured Kenyans were walking around aimlessly, in shock, crying ...; dreadful scene [with] dead people being removed from all over. Scores of people were cut by flying glass as the blast shattered windows in office buildings five blocks away. U.S. Ambassador Prudence Bushnell, who was in a building two doors away from the Embassy, was slightly injured ..., embassy officials said (1).

Less than an hour after the explosion, thousands of ordinary citizens had crowded around the embassy building. As if called to duty, these volunteers descended on top of the building after the smoke had settled. The goal of that collective action was to save lives, if possible. With bare hands, they removed the blocks of stones mangled in the steel wires. It was a difficult task working without tools; something more powerful than the tools kept the unskilled and barehanded folks on top there. It is the potent instinct—the emotion that has the tendency to unleash energy in humans to move mountains, so to speak.

The attempt to rescue the victims by ordinary citizens largely occurred before the professional rescue teams arrived. However, upon their arrival, the nature of the operations was immediately transformed. As a *Washington Post* reporter observed:

> On Friday, it was a disaster zone aswarm with volunteers scrambling over broken concrete and waving frantically to direct help to half-buried survivors. Today, rope cordons went up and volunteers were directed by trained search and rescue teams that had filed out of cargo planes at Jomo Kenyatta International Airport. Among them was an Israeli urban rescue team that arrived from Tel Aviv bearing hydraulic equipment, sensitive listening devices, stretchers and dogs trained to find corpses (2).

The cordoning off of the incident scene coincided with my arrival at the scene with the late Mr. Kamau, a former Peace Corps driver. We had heard of the news in Loitoktok, a sleepy town at the foothills of Mt. Kilimanjaro where we had gone to appraise a site for volunteer placement. We arrived at the scene almost five hours after the blast. By that time, the smoke from the bombed embassy and Ufundi House still turned the often-bright Nairobi skies into an evening-like scene. What I witnessed was chilling and debilitating. For the first couple of minutes, I felt dizzy as adrenaline ran through my body while at the same time I imagined the possible deaths of everyone I knew, including many close friends. It had barely been two years since I served as chairman to all the 638 Foreign Service National employees (FSNs) who worked at the embassy, the Library of Congress, Voice of America, and the US Agency for International Development (USAID). Moreover, I used to work inside the public affairs section of the embassy and occasionally had meetings or came in to sort out human resource issues almost weekly. It was a difficult scene to bear even for a few minutes.

Several minutes after I had gathered courage, I walked toward the northern entrance of the embassy that was not much affected by the blast except for broken windows. My goal was to get inside and assist any of the survivors. Unfortunately, I was refused by the marines who had secured the perimeter and were holding guard.

By that time, around 5:00 p.m., there was only one earthmover attempting to remove the pile of debris that continued to squeeze the breath out of the victims who may have been still alive. Soon after the Israeli rescuers arrived, the US "Marines kept the crowd at bay, swiftly erected black cloth around the embassy fence and focused their efforts on the embassy. Their action led to charges by scores of volunteers that the Americans were only interested in their own citizens and were not concerned with the Kenyan dead and injured in the [Ufundi] building next door (3)."

Whether rightly or wrongly misplaced reactions, the marines were probably following the procedures occasioned by such incidents. One view is that by cordoning off the site, operations by professionals were made much easier. The other view is that they were trying to preserve clues for the probable cause of the incident for later investigations. Moreover, I surmised that at all times during such incidents, the marines must try to secure classified information. To the ordinary people on the streets, the cordoning off was misunderstood to mean that the marines did not care about the lives of those who might have been still alive even in the face of active rescue operations. It is in the same vein that the local papers later claimed that the American rescuers were more concerned about the lives of their own people at the embassy. This contradicts the fact that there were more Kenyan employees inside the embassy than the Americans either before or at the time of the incident.

Days after the rescue teams and the American and Kenyan government officials had had the chance to account for all the dead by reviewing data from Nairobi's hospitals, a family continued to search for a single mother of three—for she could not be found in any of the hospitals or morgues. She was a woman named Rose Wanjiku. Kenyans and the international media based in Nairobi at that time cannot afford to forget her story, nor her resiliency to keep on breathing under the rubble. Nearly a week (sixty hours or so) after the incident, Rose still had the energy to make sounds of desperation—sounds of "Please," it might have seemed, "do not let me die." To be precise, and according to the Israeli rescuers at the collapsed Ufundi House under which she was buried, Rose was heard for days tapping from beneath the rubble. As the story kept being relayed on the local TV channels, tears rolled down the cheeks of the emotional and the caring residents. In a powerful display of volunteerism, ordinary Kenyans joined the Israeli rescuers to remove by hand the mountain-like rubble of the collapsed Ufundi House where Rose was trapped. The volunteers are reported to have stayed days and nights at the site to talk to the invisible Rose, hoping that would sustain her energy and will for survival. Unfortunately, after days of hard work and exasperation, the rescue team could no longer hear Rose's voice or her tapping. In short, she no longer responded when her name was called out. Rose finally succumbed. Nonetheless, her persistent cry from beneath the rubble is reminiscent of the story of Rachel in the Bible that reads:

> A voice is heard in Ramah, weeping and great mourning, Rachel weeping for her children and refusing to be comforted, because they are no more. (Mathew 2:18, Holy Bible, International Version 1984)

Before her tapping and voice finally faded, it was as if Rose was weeping for all the dead in the Ufundi Building, the Cooperative House, the American embassy, and on the streets. After Rose went on to the afterlife, many of us in the nation's capital at the time retreated into our homes with eyes glued to local news reports to count the dead. The official figures later released by the US State Department indicated a total of 213 lives lost in that single incident. The majority, 94 percent (201), were Kenyans (including employees of the embassy and members of the general public who were at the wrong place at the wrong time), with the remaining 6 percent (12) being Americans. The total figure was later revised upward to 218; their names are engraved on the Memorial Park stone at the very site where the embassy once stood. The embassy has since then been moved away from downtown Nairobi.

Other Global Examples

Several incidents in which ordinary people have made significant contributions toward rescue operations continue to be documented in print and electronic media reports. Consider the following incidents in which untrained bystanders attempted to save lives of those caught in catastrophic events. In these cases, the bystanders either acted alone or assisted professionals with rescue operations in emergency situations.

Consider the mine explosion of 1904 that occurred at Allegheny Coal Company in Harwick, Pennsylvania (Wooster, 2000, 2005), which killed 181 people. Immediately after the incident, engineer Selwyn Taylor went into the mine and rescued one miner; Selwyn later died from inhaling poisonous gasses during the rescue. A volunteer by the name of Daniel Lyle died after he attempted to help several survivors to the surface. Another show of compassion and bravery by ordinary citizens, regardless of potential risk, took place in Denmark on April 9, 1940. On that fateful day, the Germans invaded Denmark and Norway. Their immediate goal was to capture all the Jews and send them to concentration camps. After being informed by a sympathetic German diplomat, ordinary citizens provided protection to the Jews by hiding them before they could be clandestinely led into the neighboring Sweden. That sign of bravery in the face of possible ruthless Nazi retaliation resulted in a thoughtful film, *Rescue in Scandinavia*. It depicts what Margaret Walden calls "moral courage" (*Printable Teacher's Guide—Rescue in Scandinavia*, n. d., p. 1). In her own words:

> [It is the] … recollections and interpretations of ordinary people who provided extraordinary assistance to others in desperate need. The film centers on the comments of people who, in their own words, acted as individuals to help individuals, for no reason other than it was the right thing to do. 'Rescue in Scandinavia'

portrays—in the word of some of the participants in this effort, and in archival footage—the urgency of the rescue activities and the selfless manner in which they were undertaken in spite of the risks to the rescuers. The moral courage of the rescuers is clearly distinguished from the inhumanity of the persecutors and the indifference of the bystanders.

In another incident, it was private taxis and newspaper delivery vans that transported the injured and the dead to nearby medical care centers following a fire that burned the Coconut Grove Night Club in Boston in 1942 (Scanlon 2011). A similar episode took place in the Province of Alberta, Canada, in 1987. Immediately after a tornado destroyed homes in Edmonton, it was the local residents who used their cars as ambulances to take the injured to medical care facilities. Two years later, on October 17, 1989, after a 7.1 magnitude earthquake struck Loma Prieta near the Santa Cruz Mountains in the San Francisco area, ordinary citizens worked "with firefighters to stretch fire hoses from the waterfront to burning buildings" (Wooster, 2000, 2005). A total of sixty-two people were killed, and 3,757 were injured in that incident.

When a major earthquake with a magnitude of 8.0 struck Mexico City on the morning of September 19, 1985, killing over ten thousand people, as many as eight hundred victims were saved by brave ordinary citizens who spontaneously responded to the incident long before professional rescuers were brought in from various Mexican cities as well as from the international community. Soon after the incident, a number of youths organized themselves into brigades that crawled beneath collapsed structures and through the rubble to look for survivors. They further organized makeshift ambulances to ferry the injured to hospitals and provided food, shelter, and emotional support. Despite losing one hundred lives of their own, in 1986 this informal group of volunteers later transformed into the Civil Protection Committee. With the support of government, the group is today considered one of the most elite rescue teams in Mexico and beyond. They have, for example, provided rescues to earthquake victims in countries such as Haiti, Taiwan, and Costa Rica.

A study conducted by Marla Petal et al. (2004) remarkably shows that 93 percent of those who were trapped following Italy's 1980 earthquake were rescued by volunteers without any relevant skills. They used ordinary tools to provide assistance. In another similar incident in Tangshan city in northern China, an earthquake struck in the early hours of July 28, 1976, killing over 240,000 and leaving more than 164,000 injured. Immediately following the earthquake, the injured were able to crawl out to rescue 80 percent of those still under the rubble. This proves that whenever disasters happen, people show not only their empathy but also an outpouring of altruism. Again, it is as if humans are naturally wired to save lives of our own species, protecting human DNA from extinction.

The 1990s also saw its share of catastrophes. In 1992, a sewer exploded in Guadalajara, Mexico. As soon as it happened, nearby ordinary citizens organized themselves into search and rescue teams. Through group efforts and ingenuity, they were able to "siphon air to those who were entrapped" by using simple tools and household hoses (Wesley and Kransnov 2005, p. 26). The following year, on September 22, 1993 at 2:58 a.m., an Amtrak train with 220 passengers and eighteen crew members derailed in the US state of Alabama. It was the survivors who provided first aid until the rescue team arrived nearly two hours later. Investigators concluded that nearly fourteen passengers would have perished had it not been for the efforts of their fellow travelers. On January 17, 1995, when Japan experienced one of the deadliest earthquakes to hit the Osaka-Kobe metropolitan area, measuring 7.3 on the Richter scale, only 25 percent of the survivors were rescued by experts and a mere 26 percent transported in the official vehicles of professional rescuers. The remainder (74 percent) were transported in private automobiles (Wessley and Krasnove, 2005). In fact, Wessley and Krasnove report that civilians responded long before professional rescue teams arrived and were able to provide more assistance than the professionals after the incident. Over 5,500 people lost their lives in that incident, yet this number would have been higher had it not been for the efforts of civilian responders (*Encyclopedia Brittanica* 2015).

At 10:30 p.m. on September 2, 1998, Swiss Air flight 111 crashed into the Atlantic Ocean near Halifax International Airport in Nova

Scotia after smoke was reported coming out of the engine and the plane was therefore cleared to land at the nearest airport. After the crash in the shallow water off Peggy's Cove, it was the local fishermen in their boats who first responded, led the search for survivors, and provided the needed assistance (CBC News, 2013; Scanlon, 2011). The plane had taken off from John F. Kennedy Airport in New York and was bound for Geneva, Switzerland. To close the decade, in 1999, a French village was buried by 300,000 cubic meters of snow. The rescue operations were conducted entirely by local citizens because specialists could not reach the site (National Geographic Channel, n. d.).

Black swan events such as those already cited above never seem to end. Just over a decade into the twenty-first century, the number of natural and man-made catastrophes has been overwhelming—including hurricanes, tornadoes, shipwrecks, mass murders by lunatics, earthquakes, and plane crashes. In a number of these cases, ordinary citizens have demonstrated heroic acts in an attempt to save lives. I recount some of them below.

1. *Air France Airbus A-340-313, Flight 358, Toronto International Airport*

   On August 2, 2005, a plane with 297 passengers and twelve crew that had taken off from Paris with Toronto as its destination overshot the runway and ended up in a ravine. The crash into the ravine was followed by a fireball. All passengers were safely evacuated with only twelve sustaining minor injuries. According to a *New York Times* report (Fischhoff, 2005, August 7), "once out of the wreckage, they were aided by other strangers who, on the spur of the moment and no expertise in emergency situations, had pulled off a nearby highway and calmly charged into the scene, despite the risks posed by an exploding plane." The *Times* report added that "in such incidents people 'almost keep their wits and elevate their humanity." Similar reports confirmed that soon after the plane ran off the runway, it was the ordinary citizens who used their cars to take the traumatized passengers to various destinations, although the plane had not been cleared at customs (*Tribune*, 2005; Scanlon, 2011).

2. *Haiti Earthquake*

When a devastating 7.0 magnitude earthquake hit the impoverished Caribbean nation of Haiti on January 12, 2010, killing more than 200,000 people, the world reacted immediately by sending in medical and rescue teams. Despite all their equipment and expertise, by the time the rescuers reached the mangled and remote scenes, they were able to save only 211 trapped victims, according to Dr. Isaac Ashkenazi, a world expert on disaster response and crisis leadership (Herman, 2011). Meanwhile, thousands of other victims were saved by the Haitian citizens themselves—unhurt or at least ambulatory bystanders who risked their own lives to pull others out of the rubble. In reaction to the positive response by ordinary people, Ashkenazi observed that "the real first responders are not the official-with-uniform first responders ... The real first responders are the bystanders" (Herman, 2011, September 12). In the aftermath, ordinary people used basic tools at their disposal to save lives.

3. *Pakistan and Afghanistan Avalanches*

In 2010, villagers digging with sticks and spades rescued seven survivors from an avalanche that slammed into a remote village in northern Pakistan, killing up to thirty people, officials said. The disaster struck in Kohistan district, which borders Pakistan's mountainous northern areas and where heavy snow and treacherous winter weather prevented rescuers from reaching the stricken area quickly. A massive wall of snow plowed into the small village of Bagroodara wedged into a mountain in the Kundian valley, where poor communication links meant it had taken up to twelve hours for appeals for help to filter through. Local residents reached the scene first, and police arrived more than twenty-four hours after the avalanche hit, according to the senior police officer, Mohammad Ilyas in Dasu of the main town in Kohistan. "They were ill-equipped, but using local tools like spades and sticks, residents joined police and recovered seven people alive," he said. The village is in Kohistan district, about

220 kilometers north of the Pakistani capital Islamabad. "We have serious communication problems. Sometimes it takes 12 hours for people to convey information," Mr. Ilyas said. "They travel by foot; there is no other way. Today we have sent helicopters to assist with the rescue" (ABC News/AFP, 2010, February 20). In a related incident in March 2012, rescuers shoveled through deep snow in search of victims of an avalanche that destroyed a village of two hundred people in northeastern Afghanistan. People from a nearby village were the first to reach the site and were joined by rescue workers from Darwaz district who walked for two days to reach the remote area.

4. *Virginia Beach Helicopter Crash*

Following a US Navy jet crash into apartment buildings in Virginia Beach on Friday, April 5, 2012, various newspapers and national television newscasts reported the extent to which ordinary citizens, who happened to be nearby at the time of the incident, assisted with initial rescue efforts. For example, one of the local residents pulled the pilot away from the fire to safety. Additionally, when the firefighters arrived on the scene, they were aided by neighbors, some of whom held the water hoses. The following passages recount citizens' demonstrations of potent instinct, which were highly commended by Virginia's authorities and trained experts:

We saw neighbors rushing to the assistance of neighbors, the Navy pilots waiting until the very last second to eject, citizens pulling the pilots to safety and treating them, and a successful and efficient coordinated response from the first responders, the city and others," McDonnell [the State Governor] said. "It was the very best of Virginia on display." Among those who sprang into action was an off-duty Coast Guard member. Petty Officer 2nd Class Nick Beane was at a friend's house having lunch when the jet went down, according to a statement from the Coast Guard. "My training kicked in," Beane said. "I saw fire and explosion, and I knew I had to help." He ran to nearby building and knocked on doors to make sure everyone was outside. He then saw one of the pilots, lying on the ground near flames." With the help of a civilian, they cut the pilot loose from his parachute and carried him to safety. The Coast Guard said, "his own safety was the last thing on his mind." (CNN Staff Writer, 2012)

It was residents, not emergency officials or sailors, who pulled the two aviators to safety away from the flames. The videos taken immediately after the crash showed neighbors hoisting fire hoses to help firefighters put out the blaze. Even Adm. John C. Harvey, commander of US Fleet Forces, praised the cooperative effort when he stated, "That was absolutely evident in how we worked together as a collective body to work through this incident" (Associated Press, 2012).

5. *Auto Accident—Utah, United States*

On September 13, 2011, there was an incident involving a motorcyclist on a major highway near Utah State University in the US state of Utah. The rider was trapped beneath a vehicle that collided with another, resulting in a fireball. Ordinary citizens, including students and others nearby, rushed to the scene and pulled the motorcycle rider to safety.

The report further states that the rescuers ran to a nearby facility to get a fire extinguisher, which they, together with a state trooper, used efficiently to extinguish the fire, thus saving one person's life. According to Jeff Garff's video of the incident, "several startled bystanders [looked] under the BMW as flames [leapt] into the air." A CNN Wire staff added that the crowd quickly grew "to include a man in a suit, construction workers wearing hard hats, a woman in sandals and a young man carrying a backpack. After one person in the group [tried] to pick up the blazing car, the crowd [joined] in and [lifted] the 4,000-pound vehicle" (CNN, 2011, September 13). Another report compiled by Mathew K. Jensen (2012, September 13) narrated the entire incident as follows.

Police and fire authorities are praising the heroic work of a dozen bystanders who pulled a man from beneath a burning car in Logan on Monday morning. At about 11:45 a.m., an eastbound motorcycle rider took evasive action to avoid colliding with a BMW sedan that was pulling out from a parking lot on the south side of U.S. Highway 89 across from Utah State University's Lund Hall. The two vehicles impacted and erupted into flames, trapping the male rider underneath the burning car. Meanwhile, students and at least two construction workers who saw the crash rushed over to help. "We lifted the side of the car up, and some other guys pulled him from underneath," said Ben Wilson of Mount Sterling, a construction worker at the school's new agricultural building. The group lifted the passenger side of the sedan off the roadway while a man pulled the victim's legs to free him from the fiery wreck. "They're rescuers," said Assistant Police Chief Curtis. "They did a great job getting him out and getting him the help he needed ... I'm impressed that that many people would get involved and risk their own safety," Curtis added. Assistant Logan Fire Chief Brady Hansen said bystanders also helped to put out the vehicle fire. Police officers and construction crews grabbed fire extinguishers from nearby buildings to help get the flames out.

6. *Dana Airline Disaster, Nigeria*
    Another rare catastrophe that is more devastating than road or rail accident in its effects is a plane crash. In these cases, it is

difficult to imagine that there would be any room for ordinary people eager to assist with rescue to actually do so. Plane crashes often end up in virulent infernos, especially when they crash on land and not in the sea. On June 3, Nigeria's Dana Airline with 153 on board crashed into a two-story building in the city of Lagos after a short flight from Abuja, the capital (Agoi, 2012). All the 153 passengers perished in that incident. It was also reported that ordinary citizens willingly gave support to the firefighters by holding on to the water hoses (Akintunde, Akinleye, Reuters, 2012).

7. *Potomac River Air Crash, United States*

Another air crash occurred on January 13, 1982, in Washington, DC, in which bystanders and survivors attempted a most treacherous rescue operation. After taking off from Washington, DC's, National Airport in freezing winter weather, Air Florida flight 90, on its trip to Tampa and Fort Lauderdale, crashed onto the Fourteenth Street Bridge over the Potomac River (Kaye, n. d.). On impact, the plane crashed into six cars and a truck before it plunged into the icy river. A few minutes after the incident, two brave bystanders attempted a most daring rescue before formal rescue personnel arrived thirty-five minutes after the incident. First was Roger Olian, who jumped into the icy water in an attempt to save at least one or more of the victims. About fifty yards into the river, his body succumbed to the numbness, and he couldn't move any further; observers had to move him back to the shore. The second bystander rescuer was Lenny Skutnik. He reportedly removed his cowboy boots and jumped into the icy river that a few minutes earlier had restrained Roger Olian. He focused his attention on a survivor, Priscilla Tirado, whom he was able to bring ashore. She lived but lost her baby and her husband, who were among the seventy-four dead passengers. Additionally, one survivor, Arland Williams, is said to have kept passing the helicopter rescue rope on to others but never had the chance to use it to save his own life. The actions by these three individuals corroborate observations by John Drury and Stephen Reicher (2010) that "in disasters [such as the Air Florida incident], people are more likely to be killed by compassion than competition … In emergencies, people don't panic. In fact, they show a remarkable ability to organize themselves and support one another (p. 1)."

8. *Child Rescued from Fire, United States*
On March 26, 2010, in Louisville, Kentucky, a twenty-two-year-old woman, Alyson Myatt, risked her life to save a five-year-old boy, Aden Hawes, who was trapped in his room as an inferno gutted the house. Ms. Myatt, who was in another room at the time, ran barefoot to the room that was hundreds of degrees Fahrenheit. Ms. Myatt sustained third-degree burns and was treated at the Louisville University Hospital. After the incident, officials said, "There's no question that Myatt's fearless actions saved Aden's life and allowed him to come through the experience unscathed" (Celizik, 2010, p. 26).

9. *Man Saves Eight While His Family Dies, China*
When a huge fire broke out in Shitou Street in West Lake District, Nanchang City, China, at 4:00 a.m., on November 24, 2011 (ChinaHush, 2011), a fifty-two-year-old man, Xiong Niaobao, ran past a helpless crowd watching the inferno that had engulfed several houses and shouted, "Don't hold me, I will go save them." He went from door to door, yelling, "Fire! Wake up!" Unfortunately, the members of his family died because after he woke up his wife and mother-in-law, he never had the chance to go back and ensure that they were out of danger. Xiong saved a total of eight people, two of whom were a deaf couple.

10. *Man Loses His Life after Rescuing Drowning Family, China*
In the afternoon of July 3, 2012, a twenty-seven-year-old man named Deng Jinjie was walking his dogs by Sunshuihe River when he heard a cry for help by a family of three who was swimming.

Their child was being swept downstream, and they were in no position to help. Deng responded to the distress by jumping into the river without taking off his pants or shoes. After rescuing the child and the parents, Deng was nowhere to be seen. Apparently, he had lost the strength to get himself back to the bank of the river. Others, together with the Loudi City Fire Department, tried to recover Deng, who was found dead.

11. *Sandy Hook Elementary School Shooting, United States*
On the morning of December 14, 2012, the town Newton, Connecticut, woke up to a horrific incident that took the nation by surprise. A twenty-year-old man, Adam Lanza, forced his way into two classrooms of Sandy Hook Elementary School where six- to seven-year-old children had just begun their learning. At about 9:30 a.m., Adam walked into the first classroom where fourteen children and their substitute teacher, Lauren Rousseau, were already settled in for the day's activities. He opened fire, killing them all. He then moved to the second classroom where first graders were with their teacher, Victoria Soto, twenty-seven, and killed all of them as well. On hearing the gunshots outside of her classroom, Soto had quietly moved her students away from the door and tried to hide her kids in a closet. Investigators said that Soto's action of moving the kids away from the door enabled some of the children to flee to safety even though others didn't make it.

Another teacher, Annie Marie Murphy, was shot dead while shielding children from the gunshots. Other acts of heroism included that of Laura Feinstein, who gathered some of the children under her arms and hid under computer desks and shelves and tried calling 911, only to be failed by lack of network; she managed to text her husband. The principal and school psychologist, who heard the sound of gunshots from the meeting room, braved their way into the hallway to determine what was going on; Lanza shot all of them before committing suicide with a bullet in his head (Winter, 2014; CNN, 2014).

12. *Fire at the Boate Kiss Nightclub, Brazil*

At about 2:00 a.m. on January 27, 2013, a fire broke out at Kiss Nightclub in Brazil's southern city of Santa Maria. The fire was ignited by fireworks performed on stage by the band. The acoustic insulation caught fire, and the scene descended into chaos, causing about two thousand revelers to run for safety. Most of them, students from the Federal University of Santa Maria, ran to the only exit but were initially barred by guards, who mistakenly thought some were trying to leave without paying. However, when they sensed danger, they left the door open. With the panic, many fell to the ground and were trampled. A survivor, Pamella Vedovotto, recalls a Mr. Rafael De Oliveria who grabbed her and rushed her toward the exit. Oliveria went back to save others but did not make it back alive (Shasta, 2013; Schwirtz, 2013). Volunteers are reported to have assisted police and firefighters by using axes and sledgehammers to break the windows so that survivors could escape. The incident reminds us of a similar incident in the US city of West Warwick, Rhode Island, in which fireworks (pyrotechnic display) by the Great White Band on the night of February 20, 2003, caused an inferno that killed a hundred partygoers at the Station Nightclub. One of the survivors, Erin Pucino, later told the press that she owed her life to one of the revelers who pulled her out to safety (CNN. com/US, 2003). The rescue of Erin and others happened minutes before firefighters and paramedics arrived at the scene.

13. *Lifeguard Violates Rule to Save a Drowning Man, United States*

In June 2012, a lifeguard named Thomas Lopez ran to save a drowning man at Hallandale Beach, Florida. Lopez responded to the call based on his training and ran to the scene. He provided the needed assistance and put the man, who had turned blue, in an appropriate position before an off-duty nurse came to provide assistance before the paramedics came. The management for whom Lopez worked accused him of violating the company rule of not leaving his designated area, thereby putting beachgoers in his Hallandale section in danger during his brief absence. It was, therefore, a case of liability had something happened to the man. Lopez said, "It was a long run, but someone needed my help. I wasn't going to say no" (*Sun Sentinel*, 2012, June 3; CNN, 2012, July 5). The action, however, cost him his job with Jeff and Associates.

This comes as a surprise to those of us who have strong faith in the training of professional rescuers. The action by the lifeguard's employer raises an ethical issue: Is there a boundary for saving a human life? What is the right thing to do where existing rules prohibit a lifesaving action outside of a job's physical boundary, in the name of accountability? Following the report, a blogger posted a comment of interest, "to punish a guard trained to save fellow human beings [in] distress—even [when] off the boundary … Where is a boundary line in saving a person's life." Perhaps for some there is a boundary, but from where the blogger sits or stands, corroborated with research findings, humans will let their potent instincts flow freely and attempt, whenever feasible, to save a life. In fact, it feels awkward not trying to do something about an incident as Lopez did. It is like we have this duty of helping those in distress added to our lives (Amy Okoth, personal communication, 2012).

14. *The Batman Movie Incident, United States*
    In another selfless act of bravery driven by potent instinct, three young American men died taking bullets for their girlfriends. In an incident that stunned the United States on July 20, 2012, James Holmes shot at random people in Aurora (Colorado) Movie Theater during a midnight premiere of *The Dark Knight Rises*, leaving twelve people dead and several injured. In a quick reaction to the bloodthirsty gunman, Jon Blunk, Matt McQuinn, and Alex Teves pushed their girlfriends to the floor under the seats

and threw their bodies on top of each girlfriend to shield them from the gunshots. Each of these selfless men died on the spot at the now infamous "*Batman* movie theater" (Judith Crosson, Kerry Wills, and Bill Hutchinson, *New York Daily News*, 2012, July 21). Exactly one month after the *Batman* movie massacre, bystanders jumped onto the train tracks at the Kendal Station in Boston, Massachusetts, during an evening rush hour to rescue a woman carrying her four-year-old son, both of whom had fallen onto the tracks (FoxNews.com, 2012, August 23).

15. *Girls' Education Crusader, Malala, Shot in Pakistan*
Consider the case of a fourteen-year-old Malala Yousafzai, a Pakistani girl shot in the head and neck in an assassination attempt by the Taliban. Malala had been inside a bus on the way home from school. She was shot because of her persistent call for the promotion of girls' education, something deeply condemned by the Taliban (Malm, 2012, October 9). A day after being hospitalized at the Saidu Sharif Teaching Hospital in the Swat Valley in the northwest region of Pakistan, hundreds of ordinary people queued at the hospital to donate blood in order to save her life. The widespread humanitarian response that followed the incident, including that of the government of the United Arab Emirates that airlifted the girl to a specialty hospital in Birmingham in the United Kingdom for treatment, reminds us of a statement by American president Thomas Jefferson, "Every human mind feels pleasure in doing good to another" (in Sabato, 2007, p. 10). Fortunately, by the time of writing this section (May, 2015), Malala had already recovered, became the youngest person ever to win the Nobel Peace Prize, and continues with her own schooling in addition to promoting girls' education on a global scale, thanks to the pleasure of those who came to her rescue.

16. *Girls' Dormitory Burning, Kenya*
The innate human instinct to assist others in distress was exemplified on August 23, 2012, by villagers in Homa Bay

County in Western Kenya. In the middle of the night, the villagers responded to cries for help in the nearby St. Theresa's Asumbi Girls' Boarding Primary School, where fire had gutted a dormitory with several young girls sleeping inside. Although a watchman at the school denied them entry, the villagers forced their way in and broke the outside padlock of the hostel. By forcing the locked door open, one girl's life was saved even though eight others died. According to newspaper reports, the girls lost their lives because the only door they could use to escape was locked from the outside. Moreover, the windows were reinforced with strong metal bars and wire mesh, making it impossible for any of the victims to exit from the looming danger (*Standard Digital Reporter*, 2012).

17. *Hurricane Sandy, United States*

When superstorm Sandy hit New Jersey and several eastern seaboard states the last week of October 2012, many homes were destroyed and as many 230 people or more lost their lives. Despite these tragic losses, the story of Mike and how he was saved and cared for by a Good Samaritan is worth sharing. After his house was marooned with almost ten feet of water, Mike of Toms River, New Jersey, broke into an empty house owned by a woman who had evacuated before the hurricane hit. He looked for a blanket or anything to keep hypothermia away. According to Mike's note quoted below, he thought he was on the verge of death until a stranger came to his rescue.

Whoever reads this, I'm dying. I am 28 yrs. old my name is Mike. I had to break in to your house. I took blankets off the couch, I have hypothermia. I didn't take anything. A wave threw me out of my house down the block. I don't think I'm going to make it. The water outside is 10 ft. deep at least. There is no rescue. Tell my dad I love him and tried getting out. His number is ###-###-#### his name is Tony. I hope you can read this I'm in the dark.

I took a black jacket too. Goodbye. God all mighty help me (nbc.newyork.com, 2012)

Mike was later discovered by a stranger named Frank, who took him into his home and gave him not only shelter but clothes and food as well. This story is interesting because of the mention of no professional rescuers at hand. Second, the fact that when an incident such as this happens, it is often the neighbors and survivors who will provide immediate assistance. Professional rescuers cannot at be every spot, given institutional centrality. Firefighters and ambulances are always stationed at particular locations and therefore cannot easily respond when emergencies such as flood and tornadoes wreak widespread havoc.

18. *Ferry Disaster, South Korea*
On the fateful day of April 16, 2014, MV *Sewol*, a South Korean ferry, capsized with 476 passengers, of whom 340 were secondary school students. The ferry was traveling from the Port of Incheon to the resort island of Jeju. Immediately after the sighting of the incident, some of the victims were rescued by fishing boats and the crew in commercial vessels. The South Korean Coast Guard, Navy ships, and helicopters arrived about thirty minutes later (*Guardian*, April 28). It was reported by the same paper on April 28 that about five thousand volunteers had participated in the rescue (Harlan, 2014).

19. *Couple Rescued from Burning Car, United States*
At around 3:00 p.m. on Sunday, May 17, 2015, a head-on collision on a North Carolina road resulted in a fiery explosion. William Thompson and his wife, Kathleen, became trapped inside their Acura. Newspaper reports indicate that a number of neighbors sprang into action as heavy smoke and flames engulfed the other car, a Chrysler SUV, and threatened the Acura as well. Everett Bacon, who lived nearby, grabbed several fire extinguishers from his home and started fighting the flames before firefighters

arrived. Another off-duty officer, Captain Steve Voglezon, who was on his way to a mall with his girlfriend, ran to the scene to assist. He used a fire extinguisher to break the windows of the Acura and rescued the couple. During an interview, the captain said, "I picked up the other gentleman, took him to safety, while the officer was trying to free the other woman on the other side of the vehicle." Also at the scene was John Spurrell, who lived nearby. He reportedly helped rescue one of the victims from his burning Chrysler before grabbing his cell phone to start recording the scene (*Lloyd*, 2015, May 18).

20. *Train Derailment, United States*

Shortly after 9:00 p.m. on May 12, 2015, Amtrak train 188 derailed in north Philadelphia on its way to New York City from Washington, DC. Immediately after the crash, and before professional rescuers arrived, the survivors helped each other to safety. Consider the assistance provided by these two individuals: former congressman Patrick Murphy and Max Helfman. Murphy, with a military background, provided all the help he could. He said in an interview, "We have an ethic in the military, you know, we leave no one behind and I wasn't going to climb out when there were people hurting." A mother, Joan Helfman, said this of her son Max: "He got me out of the train that was filled with smoke, but he said, 'Mom, I have to go back and get everyone else out.'" Max himself had this to say, "I was in a position where I could help them, so I don't know, instinctively, that is what I did." The derailment left eight dead and more than two hundred injured (CBS News, 2015).

21. *First Responders Save Road Accident Victims, Vietnam*
Enforcement of speed limits in Vientiane, the capital and the largest city of Laos, is generally considered weak. Road fatalities are therefore commonplace, particularly individuals on motorbikes. The city has the highest road toll per capita in Asia

(Barker, ABC News). Out of compassion and due to inadequate government response to such emergencies, ordinary citizens (i.e., teenagers, students, housewives, and shopkeepers) with no training or background in emergency response have formalized their rescue assistance to road victims as they occur. Operating from a rented house close to a major highway, the volunteers who call their operation Vientiane Rescue respond to emergencies in a donated old 4WD vehicle. Once on scene, they check for vital signs, bandage any bleeding wounds, and take the injured or the dead to the nearest hospital in the city. The rescue team will then remove the bandage once the body has been released to the hospital staff, sanitize the bandage in soapy water, and head back to the road where it can help another wounded victim. These first responders' have no resources or training to provide any serious rescue. However, what is key here is their drive to assist regardless of their inadequacy. As Barker aptly commented, "They're the most inspiring people—big hearts, they just love helping those in need, even if it means putting their own safety at risk for a stranger."

22. *Armenian Swimmer Hero Saves Lives*

On September 16, 1976, an Armenian swimmer, Shavarsh Karapetyan, was jogging along a dam in the city of Yerevan when he noticed a trolleybus that had lost control flying off into the freezing water, with ninety-two passengers on board. The bus sank to approximately thirty feet (ten meters) deep. Guided by instinct, Shavarsh leaped into the frigid water in an attempt to rescue the victims. In thirty dives, he was able to break through the bus windows and to bring alive to the surface twenty people, although not all made it. Unfortunately, he suffered pneumonia, nervous exhaustion, and blood contamination after swallowing polluted water. Shavarsh spent forty-six days in the hospital before making a recovery. In an interview by *Komsomolskaya Pravda*, a daily Russian newspaper, he made the following remarks:

It is something from above that is guiding humanity, you know something is guiding us. Because at that moment I had to be at the world championships in Hannover. But for some reason, my Visa was not ready ... so I left bitter and went training when the crash happened. (PeopleOfAR, 2014)

Nine years later, on February 19, 1985, Shavarsh was by the Soviet Armenian sports hall when he noticed that people were trapped inside by a fierce fire. Instinctively, he ran into the building and pulled some of the victims outside. He sustained severe burns and smoke inhalation resulting in his hospitalization for a long time. He received a number of awards for his heroism.

23. *Tunisia Terror Attack*
    On June 26, 2015, as the infamous Islamic State of Iraq and Syria (ISIS) beheaded factory worker Herve Cornara in Chassieu, France, another supporter of the Islamic group opened fire on Western tourists at a beach in Sousse, Tunisia. Although as many as thirty-eight people were shot dead and thirty-nine were injured, local Bellevue hotel workers formed a human shield on the beach to protect the lives of the tourists. They were quoted to have told the gunman, "You must kill us first, but we are Muslims." Another act of heroism was that of British tourist Mathew James, thirty, who was shot three times as he shielded his fiancée, Saera Wilson, from the gunman; James survived and is recovering at the time of writing this section (July, 2015). Of those who died, fifteen were Britons. Some of those who survived played dead, were shielded by the locals, or had the opportunity to escape back to the hotel (Charlton, 2015).

24. *Man Tackles Suicide Bomber to Save Lives*
    It was Thursday, November 13, 2015, when Adel Termos and his daughter were walking in an open-air market in Beirut, Lebanon. They witnessed a suicide bomber detonate with explosives. As

people scampered for safety, Adel noticed a second bomber preparing to blow himself. He immediately left his daughter to tackle the bomber to the ground. Adel lost his life soon after the bomb went off, but hundreds of lives, including that of his daughter, were saved (Itkowitz, 2015). One blogger commented on Adel's act of bravery in the following terms: "In a way, Adel Termos broke human nature of self-preservation. His heroism transcended his own life to save others. To make that kind of decision in a split second, to decide that you'd rather save hundreds than to go home to your family, to decide that the collective lives of those around you are more important than your own is something that I think no one will ever understand" (p. 1).

When Bystanders / Ordinary Citizens Offer Information

We have to admit that there are certain incidents so dangerous to render impossible any rescue even from the bravest of bystanders. Even in such situations, they will always offer some assistance. Offering information about an emergency is one such contribution. Although it is not often acknowledged, this attribute certainly demonstrates the good side of humans toward victims of emergencies. Consider the following public announcement that appeared in one of East Africa's newspapers after an attack on two US embassies (in 1998) by Al Qaeda operatives.

> **CAUTION:** Usama Bin Laden is wanted in connection with the August 7, 1998, bombings of the United States embassies in Dar-es-Salaam, Tanzania and Nairobi, Kenya. These attacks killed over 200 people. Considered armed and extremely dangerous. If you have any information concerning this person, please contact your local FBI office or the nearest U.S. Embassy or Consulate.

> **REWARD:** The United States Government is offering a reward of up to $25 million for information leading directly to the apprehension or conviction of Usama Bin

Laden. (Report of the Accountability Review Boards,
August 7, 1998, US State Department)

In this announcement, ordinary citizens are being asked to offer any kind
of information that might lead to the capture of Usama Bin Laden, the
alleged mastermind of the two blasts in Nairobi and Dar-es-Salaam, and
his five accomplices.

The statement above assumes that ordinary people have a strong
connection to their community, including information not readily
available to experts. It further suggests that citizens are naturally affected
when such events occur and therefore will freely volunteer information
to the experts.

Consider the following scenario. On October 29, 2013, a British
newspaper, the *Guardian*, reported a case in which a car is said to have
deliberately crashed into a public square in Beijing, China. The crash
left five dead and thirty-eight injured. Following the incident, Chinese
security officials put out an alert for information leading to the arrest
of the two culprits, who were identified to have come from Xinjiang
Province. There are a number of such notices in print and electronic
media that cannot exhaustively be recounted here. The idea of giving
these examples is to appreciate and to sensitize the reader of this reality:
humans do care for other humans. Their deep sense of empathy and
altruism will drive them not just to rescue those in danger but also to
willingly provide information that might lead to the arrest of criminals
who are suspected to have harmed others.

Bystander Effect: When Bystanders Fail to Assist

Bystander effect theory has been proposed by researchers in an attempt
to explain why bystanders will provide assistance to those who are in
distress and at times fail to do so in similar circumstances. Popularized
by social psychologists Bibb Latané and John Darley (1968), this theory
suggests that the presence of others potentially dissuades one from
intervening in an emergency situation. In effect, the greater the number
of bystanders in a particular location (such as in the streets of New York),
the less likely individuals will assist another in distress. The opposite is

also true. The fewer the number of people in a given place, the more likely an individual will provide assistance to another person in an emergency situation. This former stance is what Darley and Latane call the "diffusion of responsibility" (1968). People will always defer the helping of a victim to other bystanders.

There are but a few exceptions when those near an incident have at times failed to provide assistance to a person in extreme danger or who have ignored cries for help. Such incidents, however, are rare. To demonstrate this, let's revisit the case of Kitty Genovese, the twenty-eight-year-old American woman who was stabbed several times by an assailant in front of her apartment in Queens, New York, on March 13, 1964 (Gado, n. d.). After parking next to her apartment at about 3:15 a.m., she noticed someone behind her. She tried to run, but the assailant caught up with her and started to stab her with a knife. Kitty, as she was later known to the public, cried for help, "Please help me! Please help me!" The first neighbor switched on the light and noticed that Kitty was on the ground crying for help. Another witness in the same building opened his window and saw the struggle. He then shouted, "Let that girl alone." The assailant walked away, and the lights went out. The assailant then returned, found Kitty close to her apartment struggling, and stabbed her again. At this time, Kitty squealed, "I am dying!" (Gado, p. 2) Windows in the apartment opened again, and the attacker disappeared from the scene. As many as five others witnessed the ordeal from their windows. Again for the third time, the lunatic returned and stabbed Kitty several times, leaving her for dead. A neighbor finally called the police at 3:50 a.m. The assailant apparently raped Kitty after she died. After the ordeal was all over, investigators revealed that about thirty-eight people in the neighborhood observed or heard the commotion but did nothing to save Kitty's life. She died on arrival at the hospital. Analysts have attributed her death to the bystander effect in which intervention is lessened whenever there are many witnesses.

As Gado has observed, "38 witnesses felt no responsibility to act because there were so many witnesses. Each one felt that the other witness would do something" (p. 3). It has thus been contended that had Kitty been attacked in a place with fewer witnesses or with only one witness, she could have been saved. This argument resonates with a sexual abuse case in New Delhi, India, on December 16, 2012. A young woman from a school was gang-raped inside a school bus and then left on a street. Despite her cries for help, passersby in the crowded city simply ignored that call. The woman later died at a Singapore hospital after being flown there for treatment. Again, the crowd's mentality was that of avoiding the offer of personal help under the assumption that another onlooker would intervene.

Let's consider another extremely sad incident in which bystanders, as well as professional rescuers, were refused by officials to enter into a compound in which young Saudi girls were trapped in a burning dormitory. When a fire broke out in at Makkah Intermediate School No. 31 on March 11, 2002, the powerful religious (Mutaween) police stopped the girls from escaping and also prevented fire rescuers and other bystanders from getting through the gate to rescue the victims. The specialized police refused because the girls were not wearing the (appropriate) Islamic dress known as *Abaya* and *Sheila* (the headscarves). Without this required attire, the girls were considered "naked" in the eyes of the religious enforcement officers. Consequently, the girls had no option but to face the wrath of death, as showing their nakedness through uncovered hair was a much bigger sin. In Saudi Arabia, the Mutaween, officially known as the Commission for the Promotion of Virtue and Prevention of Vice, regularly enforces dress codes and sex segregation and ensures that "prayers are ... performed on time" (*BBC News*, 2011, p. 1). The fire took the lives of fifteen girls and left more than fifty with different degrees of burns (BBC News, 2002; Human Rights Watch, 2002). Although this story is as sad as that of Kitty Genovese and that of the raped Indian schoolgirl, the context was much different. In the Saudi case, the expected human instinct to help others in danger was clearly not evident in the religious officials, even in the face of young girls crying in pain and begging for help. When the guards and bystanders attempted to go through the gate to help the trapped girls, they were deterred by the religious police. Moreover, when the firefighters finally arrived, the cries of pain and looming death did not alter the deep-rooted religious principles of the guards, nor did it make them reconsider their expected duty of enforcing the law. Instead, all who attempted to help were refused entrance. This particular case demonstrates where religious principles and institutionalized policy have trampled over the natural human instinct to rescue those in distress (BBC News, 2002, March 15).

Let me now corroborate the hypothesis above with another incident that my wife and I witnessed in the city of Nairobi in 1987. One morning, my wife and I were heading for a tea break at Reinsurance Plaza when suddenly a middle-aged man with a machete appeared from Harambee Avenue, chasing an older man, whom we later learned was his father. We stopped to see what was going on, as did many others. The man chased down his father, repeatedly hacking at his father's head and shoulders as bystanders looked on. The old man subsequently fell on the sidewalk, only to receive more slaughtering until he was left dead. The police arrived to take away the killer and remove his father's body. While this particular incident confirms the hypothesis that the greater the number of bystanders, the less responsibility one feels toward one who needs help in an emergency, I argue that the nature of the situation will also determine whether onlookers will act or not act. Specifically, if bystanders judge the situation to be dangerous, then they will helplessly opt not to get involved. The Nairobi incident and Kitty's case are similar given the violent nature of the attack that may have deterred any bystanders with the urge to help. Moreover, the timing of the attack can also explain the urge to help or not to help. Kitty, for example, was attacked in the wee hours when most people would generally be scared of what is happening outside of their safety zones. As my late mother once told me back in Kenya, it is a time when devils are said to roam about and bad things happen. However, in the Nairobi incident that occurred in broad daylight, with people milling on the streets, the decision by bystanders to defer intervention to the police was rational. The situation is similar to a shootout between burglars and policemen; bystanders either ignore or run for cover.

Other explanations provided by Hoffman (1981) and McDonald et al. (2015), cited in chapter 1, come to our aid. Why did witnesses not jump into action to save Kitty in New York or the old man on the streets of Nairobi? Hoffman offers two relevant hypotheses. First is reciprocal altruism. Here it is suggested that humans are more likely to assist those in danger once we are convinced that the costs of doing so are less than what we might expect to gain by the action. In other words, the decision to intervene is determined by the degree of risk. The lower the risk, the higher the chances of intervention. We can therefore argue that the inaction in both cases was due to the perceived higher risks to a potential rescuer. In both cases, witnesses feared for their own lives.

The situation as a factor is also espoused by McDonald et al. (2015). They claim that bystanders will only decide to act or not act once they have determined the degree of certainty or ambiguity. To those who heard the cry for help by Kitty, was it real to them or was it somewhat ambiguous? Was their inaction due to the ambiguity of the situation? Is it true that the person who opened the window and shouted, "Leave that girl alone," and later called the police acted because it was clearly certain someone was being harmed? McDonald and his coauthors further suggest that the decision to intervene or not to intervene is determined by "moral responsibility belief." What is the moral intensity of the incident? Do the benefits of an intervention to the victim outweigh the costs or potential risks to the bystander? How likely is it that the intervention will relieve pain or prevent death to the victim? These are questions whose answers can potentially explain why bystanders at times find themselves ready or not ready to rescue people in life-threatening situations.

An additional idea proposed by Hoffman is kin selection (see chapter 1). As in Darwin's natural selection, the hypothesis suggests that our inclination to assist those in danger is heightened by our relatedness through kinship. It can therefore be inferred that in both Kitty and Nairobi (murder) incidents, witnesses could not quickly establish any kinship between the victim and themselves. However, this argument is somewhat weak given the number of cases in which bystanders have jumped into action to save those they neither know nor have any possible relationship with through genes.

Based on all the accounts cited above, with the exception of the cases of Kitty and the brutal murder in a Nairobi street, I maintain that ordinary citizens who happen to be near an incident in which human lives are in danger will instinctively jump in to assist when they have ascertained that doing so will save the life of a victim. This happens even when their own lives might be in danger. It is a powerful human instinct that exists within us all, whether we use it or not.

Another observation is that while instinct and rationality are necessary triggers to responding to black swans, the use of one precludes the other. For example, if you notice a family trapped in a burning car, the instinct is to run over and do all you can to rescue them from danger. However, if you stop to think of why they are involved in the accident, such as violation of speeding limit, then the chances of you providing timely rescue will be slim.

While the narratives of this chapter are actual accounts reported by newspapers and other published reports, the next chapter seeks to show the results of a survey in which a number of participants were asked to give reasons why they rescued strangers in life-threatening situations even though they were not trained and may have put their own lives in danger.

Chapter 4

Potent Instinct: What the Numbers Say

In 95% of all emergencies, the victim or bystander provides
the first immediate assistance on the scene.
—FEMA

The findings by the United States Federal Emergency Management
Agency (FEMA) suggest, "In 95 percent of all emergencies, the victim
or bystander provides the first immediate assistance on the scene." A
separate study conducted by Petal, Celep, Tuzun, and Green (2004)
found the following to be true:

> In natural disasters all over the world, it is the rule
> that during the first 72 hours, the victims have only
> themselves and those immediately around them to rely
> upon. In disaster response, the first 24 hours is called
> 'The Golden Day' for it is during this time that 80%
> of the live rescues are performed. Indeed 80% of the
> live victims recovered are extricated by neighbors and
> household members, before professional responders
> arrive on the scene. Trained emergency responders
> account for another 15% of rescue.

Although the above study by Petal et al. focused only on earthquakes, these findings are fairly consistent with other studies, including one by this author. In my study, with results discussed below, those who had been victims of a road accident said 48 percent of the rescues were provided by ordinary bystanders, 23 percent by police, 6 percent professional paramedics, and 23 percent by "other." These figures, including by Petal et al., demonstrate the indisputable, instinctive intervention by ordinary citizens who happen to be near an incident, to save the lives of those in danger. Although my educated guess is that the percentages will vary by the nature of emergency and by location (e.g., in Conakry, Guinea, versus London, England), the probability that the numbers of bystanders assisting in the first critical moments of the incident will certainly be higher than that of professional rescuers who must always dispatch from specific locations and encounter challenges of traffic and distance.

Purpose

This chapter attempts to answer the question at the heart of this book: What motivates ordinary citizens to assist others in danger even when their own lives might be at stake? Is it really the pleasure they feel when they do good to those in life-threatening situations as Thomas Jefferson once surmised, or is it for other reasons? It is my hypothesis that *potent instinct (PI) drives ordinary citizens to assist those in danger.* Potent instinct is the natural force in humans that urges altruistic reactions to assist those in life-threatening situations. As we are about to learn from the results of a survey conducted in 2012, most people report they are primarily driven by a feeling or gut instinct that cannot be easily defined. So, is there any pleasure that can be gained from assisting those in distress as Jefferson once pronounced? Another way of asking the same question is: Do people assist others caught in emergency situations to satisfy their own ego and desire to find some internal pleasure? Or is it that are we are all wired to do good anyway, and that achieving some form of pleasure isn't the goal?

While this inner drive is difficult to prove, I undertook the task to explore how this instinct directs the acts of bystanders in saving the lives of those in emergencies and other catastrophic events. Thus, in order to determine a range of factors that might directly or indirectly influence bystanders' decisions to rescue strangers involved in accidents and similar emergencies, a survey was conducted in 2012 in which 193 questionnaires were completed by participants representing twenty-eight countries. Although the survey was conducted primarily in the United States, Kenya, and United Arab Emirates, participants from twenty-eight countries were fortunately accessed due to two reasons: One, convenient sampling method in public places such as classrooms, malls, gyms, hotel lobbies, and open markets made it possible to meet people from all walks of life who were willing to complete the face-to-face surveys. Two, the United Arab Emirates, where this author spent three years in a teaching assignment, is home to expatriates from many countries, particularly from the United States, Canada, West and Eastern Europe, Australia, India, and a number of African countries, including Egypt and Ethiopia. The survey was conducted at three locations: in Kenya by a trained university graduate, while those in the United Arab Emirates and the United States—particularly in Virginia, West Virginia, and Baltimore—were administered by me.

The survey asked the following questions: 1) Have you ever been involved in an emergency situation in which your life was in danger? If yes, what was it? Who came to your immediate rescue? 2) Have you ever witnessed a disastrous incident (e.g., road accident, fire)? Did you provide any assistance? If yes, why did you assist? 3) What did you expect after your action? 4) Do you think ordinary people should assist in emergency situations? If yes, why? 5) What else would you like to add?

Study participants were also asked about their age, gender, social status, and country of birth residence.

Results:

1. *Have you ever been involved in an emergency situation in which your life was in danger? If yes, what was it? Who came to your immediate rescue?*

Forty-seven percent (47 percent) of those who responded said they have been involved in life-threatening emergencies (figure 1). Fifty-four percent (54 percent) of those who answered yes were involved in a road accident; 19 percent in a fire emergency; 9 percent in a drowning; and 18 percent in "other." When all emergencies were aggregated to determine who provided immediate response, 48 percent said they were rescued by bystanders. Assistance by police came in second with 23 percent. Contrary to the popular expectations, the paramedics (or emergency rescue professionals) were the lowest, with only 6 percent. It is important to take note that these figures would certainly be different if the survey was country-specific.

Figure 1: Emergency response

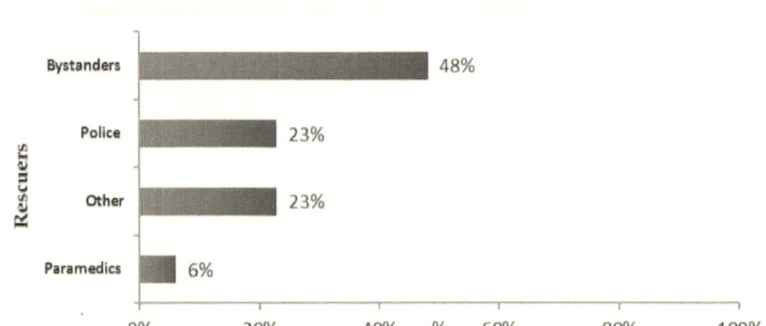

Despite this result, I would argue, based on my experience in the United States, that response by police in emergency situations is generally accompanied by firefighters and paramedics. I also want to add that, while this empirical evidence is not conclusive given the limited multisite contexts in which the study was conducted, it does give some proximate credence to the actual reality as reported in the earlier chapters of this book.

2. *Have you ever witnessed a disastrous incident (e.g., road accident, fire)? Did you provide any assistance? If yes, why did you assist?*

When the participants were asked whether they had witnessed emergency incidents, 47 percent said they had witnessed at least one or more, and 53 percent said they had not. Of those who said they had, 63 percent mentioned having provided assistance to the victims, while 37 percent did not. Another significant revelation is the reason(s) for providing such assistance. As figure 2 illustrates, the majority (71 percent) said it was the "right thing to do." Twelve (12) percent said they helped because the "victim cried for help." Seven percent did so because "paramedics were late." Another 7 percent said they moved into action because there was "no one to assist." The remaining 3 percent said they didn't know why they assisted. While I can't speak for the last group, it can be insinuated that they were driven by an instinct they cannot describe using any of the options provided.

There are several implications for these findings on a broader scale. First, the "right thing to do," with 71 percent, lends credence to the proposition put forward in the preface and the preceding chapters that natural instincts will push most people to rescue others facing imminent danger if and when possible. For example, anecdotal evidence that I assembled over time shows that about 90 percent of the people said they would jump into a swimming pool if a child accidentally slipped in, even if they were not good swimmers or didn't know whose child it was.

Other adduced evidence that is also supported by newspaper reports as narrated in chapter 2 is the response of bystanders to road accidents. These reports show how total strangers who happened to be near an accident ran to rescue accident victims. Moreover, those to whom I have informally asked this question repeat their readiness to break a window of a car involved in an accident if those inside seem to be in danger. Of course, there are exceptions. For example, in the United Arab Emirates, the law prohibits ordinary people to attempt to rescue

Figure 2: Reasons for assisting

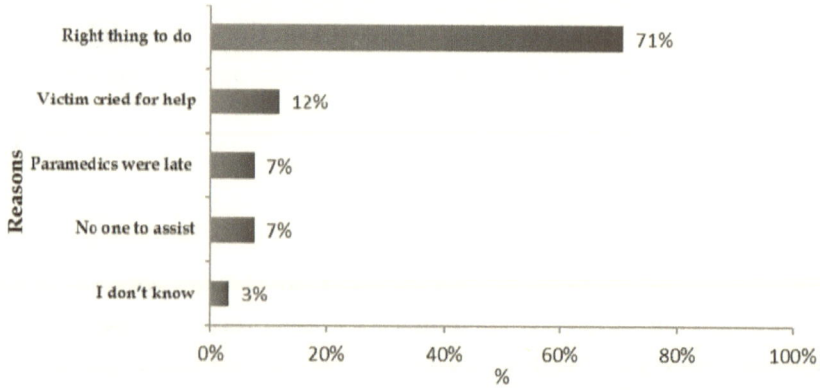

accident victims because they are not qualified and may further endanger the life of accident victims due to improper handling. Moreover, assisting others in road accidents is to some extent determined or controlled by the gender of the victim. For example, in the city of Abu Dhabi and in other emirates, it is prohibited for a male who is a nonrelative to an accident victim to rescue a female if doing so involves touching the victim. Rather, what is appropriate for the Good Samaritan (i.e., one who intends to help) to do is to call for emergency professionals such as the police and paramedics.

3. *What did you expect after your action? (motivation)*

The third question asked of participants regarded their expectations for providing the emergency assistance even when their own lives might have been in danger. Of those who responded, 89 percent said they "expected nothing after assisting." In other words, their action was driven by a potent instinct and not by any intrinsic or extrinsic rewards. As it were, it is that impulse most people would find difficult to explain. It is like saying, "I just found myself trying to help; I simply had to." Interestingly, only 6 percent said they expected some "social recognition," and a mere 3 percent said they expected a "monetary reward." (See figure 3.)

Figure 3: Expectation after assisting

4. *Do you think ordinary people should assist in emergency situations? If yes, why?*

Given the division of opinions that is often encountered when this question is asked, the findings of this study, while not conclusive, open up this topic for further debate. Additionally, it challenges those opposed to bystander involvement in emergencies to take a hard look at the various evidence cited in chapter 2.

While this is not quite surprising, judging by the narratives in chapter 2 in which men and women from all walks of life have come out to assist strangers in emergencies, the majority (96 percent) who completed the questionnaire were of the opinion that bystanders ought to assist in emergency situations; only 4 percent said no. The participants were further asked to give reasons why ordinary people not qualified in rescue operations should assist. Again it was surprising but not unexpected at the reasons given by respondents. Figure 4 illustrates the responses. Over half (59 percent) of respondents stated that involvement by ordinary people in emergencies was the "the right thing to do." The right thing to do is interpreted here to mean learned moral behavior inculcated by society. Parents, schools, religious institutions, government laws, and cultural practices generally enforce good moral behaviors that include, for the most part, doing good to others rather than harming them. Another 32 percent cited "natural instinct" as the sole force that drove them to assist those in imminent danger. Again, as few as 6 percent felt it was because paramedics were always late.

Figure 4: Why ordinary people should respond to emergencies

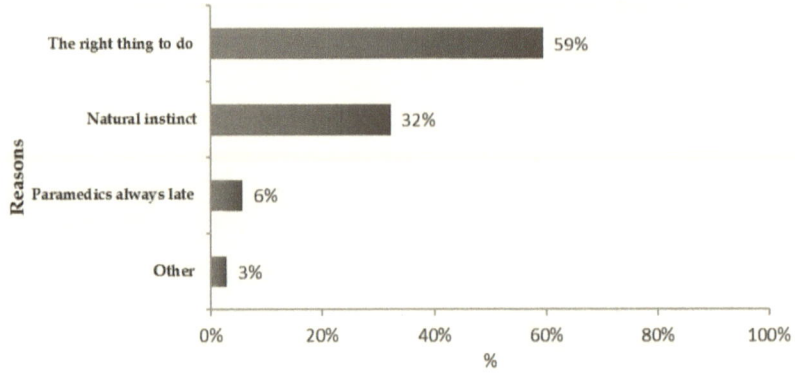

Respondents also made the following comments in relation to the question of whether nonprofessional bystanders ought to assist or not assist in emergencies. Forty percent of the expressions support immediate involvement in emergencies by ordinary bystanders. The expressions allude to our social responsibility as bystanders. Here is a summary.

a) *Social Responsibility*
- Emergencies call for collective assistance.
- Assisting others in [danger] is a moral obligation.
- It is our responsibility to help those in need.
- Ordinary people should participate for purposes of social responsibility.
- People should help each other; this makes a better society.
- Always try to assist in any emergency.
- All should be ready to give immediate help where and when required.
- It is always good to give a helping hand.
- It is the nature of all human beings to help and show concern to others.
- Ordinary people should assist in emergency situations.

- The sad part is that some people go to the disaster sites to look and not to assist.
- They could save a life before the paramedics get there.
- Willingness of heart is what we need to save a life.

b) *Emergency Policy*

Some of the participants urged the adoption of an effective national emergency response policy, as the following statements show:

- Some fear being victimized by the relatives of those rescued. Hence, there is a need for Good Samaritan laws to protect ordinary first responders.
- Sometimes ordinary people are not qualified to handle emergencies and end up killing the casualty; a law is therefore needed to state who can provide help to those involved in emergencies.
- The health sector needs to be improved [to provide better services].
- Paramedics may be late [because] facilities are limited to support their functions.

Summary

The survey results strongly suggest that humans are driven by their innate instincts to assist others in distress or in potentially harmful situations. The survey also shows that Good "Samaritanism" is partly a socially learned behavior. Therefore, helping those in a life-threatening emergency is viewed as "the right thing to do." The disparate cultures in which we live try to inculcate in us that assisting those exposed to emergencies, even if we don't know them personally, is morally appropriate or even Godly. Consequently, 71 percent of those who had assisted in emergencies said they did so because it was the right thing to do. Ninety-six percent of the survey participants were of opinion that ordinary bystanders should assist in emergency situations. Moreover, 89 percent expected nothing after assisting victims of an emergency, only 6 percent expected social recognition, and 3 percent expected a monetary reward.

Implications

- *Assistance by bystanders can be cost-effective:* Bystanders will, for the most part, be the first to witness catastrophic incidents due to proximity. Driven by human instincts, these bystanders will respond immediately in an attempt to save lives or to provide comfort to the injured. They will do this out of free will and at no cost to society. Why not incorporate them into emergency planning by providing *willing* citizens with basic lifesaving skills and training? This can be done regardless of their level of education, gender, or social status. It can be a cost-effective initiative in the long term to the nation, the community, or the household. It is however recognized that in industrialized nations, there is not much need for instituting this involvement of bystanders because effective systems are already in place, including an active role of Red Cross, among others.

- *Institutionalizing the culture of emergency preparedness:* This study builds a strong case for governments to create special agencies to coordinate and provide emergency services at the national, city/municipal, and community levels. A similar policy could support voluntary emergency response teams at community levels to complement the efforts of the relevant government agency and other bodies like the international Red Cross. This would build and nurture a culture of emergency preparedness even at the village and household levels.

- *Inclusion of ordinary citizens in emergency preparedness plan*: The concept of democratic governance calls for the inclusion of those affected by government programs in the decision-making process and the protection of their rights. Since black swans happen randomly and their impact can spread indiscriminately to any part of the society, the results of the study point to the need of including ordinary citizens to be part of the action. They can save lives or even prevent the destruction of property; they do so willingly and for free. Moreover, public administrators like firefighters and the police can capitalize on this positive energy from ordinary citizens to provide much-needed information about potential catastrophes planned by enemies of society. Ordinary citizens are privy to security information that could have helped avert the bombings of US embassies in Nairobi, Dar-es-Salaam, and New York.

The following *theory* is thus adduced from the evidence of this study:

Potent Instinct Theory (PIT)
Humans, and by extension those near an emergency, are naturally inclined to assist others in distress and will do so without expecting any form of intrinsic or extrinsic rewards; exceptions are a rarity.

This theory is promising in its ability to explain two important dimensions related to emergency response by ordinary citizens. First, PIT helps to explain the probability that bystanders (or ordinary citizens, including survivors) will respond to disastrous events to rescue victims. Second, PIT addresses why these ordinary people without any formal training in emergency rescue will jump to assist those in life-threatening situations even if they don't know the victims personally, or even when their own lives are at stake. The first dimension can thus lead the investigator to address what the bystander will do in case of an emergency, while the second facet addresses why they will move into action. Assuming this is general to the human tendency, what then are the implications for those in charge of designing policies on emergency preparedness and response? By those in charge of emergency policy, I mean agencies such as the Federal Emergence Management Agency (FEMA) in the United States, as well as city, local, and municipal governments across many nation-states. The list also includes nonprofits such as the Red Cross, whose primary goal is to design and execute emergency plans. An equally important issue that these findings and the evidence so far discussed raise is the degree to which human emotions (potent instinct) influence the timing of public policy and administrative decisions to put in place institutions/structures and laws (or plans) to mitigate, prepare, and respond to catastrophic events. The latter is the subject of chapter 4.

Before bringing this chapter to a close, it is important to recognize that some studies (Gerber, 1997; Frey et al., 2010) suggest that this natural (potent) instinct to assist victims in emergencies is anchored on socially constructed habits that are genetically wired into our system through generations. Supporters of this kind of research argue that certain human practices, like the desire to help others in need, are passed on through generations, and thus children born to grandmothers who were philanthropic will lean toward doing good as well. For example, Gerber (1997) contends that dualism between nature and culture is ingrained in our reasoning and even emotion.

In essence, the natural instinct to save lives should not be viewed purely as an autonomous actor but rather as something that is generally reinforced by social constructs that have been passed on genetically through generations. To help us better understand this relationship between society/culture and human nature (or instinct in this regard), let's borrow from the "three worlds" by Popper and Eccles (1997, cited by Gerber). Their work suggests the interconnectivity between the physical (nature or the cosmos), the mental (reasoning), and the social (culture and society). Another way to state this is the relationship between the body, the brain, and the environment that have together evolved for millennia. Any change in a member of the triage ultimately affects the other elements. Therefore, if John and Paul have this natural tendency to instinctively assist a victim of an emergency, then it ought not to be concluded that it is an action based purely on potent instinct but on the interaction between the three attributes. If this is logical, then we can almost confirm that socially constructed habits (from the environment in which we live) are part and parcel of that instinct to help those in distress. As objective reality, the society of which we are a part institutionalizes what are deemed to be good habits, such as helping. So, this insinuates that our actions, whether instinctive or not, are birthed out of customs.

Frey et al. (2010) have taken this interaction of the "three worlds" further by suggesting that there is an interplay between our survival instincts and internalized social norms. By empirically analyzing the sinking of the *Titanic* and the *Lusitania* ships, the authors found that time pressure can be a significant factor in the manner in which the affected passengers react to save others and themselves in view of impending death. For example, it was observed that it took only eighteen minutes for the *Lusitania* vessel to sink because the passengers reacted selfishly (as in the classical *homo economicus*), each to him or herself. Further research into this incident does not provide us with details with which we can further corroborate or dispute the report. What we know is that the ship was likely hit by the enemy as the nations entered into World War I. In such a scenario, it is difficult to fathom how easy or difficult it would have been for the passengers to quickly save each other from drowning. The situation was, however, different from the *Titanic* in which social behavior was exhibited by most of the passengers. They exercised a different form of rationality by assessing the situation and how they could save themselves. By forming a cohesive group in the face of life and death, the sinking of the *Titanic* was delayed to two hours, forty minutes. So what do these two sinking-vessel scenarios tell us? First, they tell us that in times of life threat, time is critical to determining how to react. Ordinarily, in the initial stages, the adrenaline will take over, thus weakening the victim facing danger or the bystander who might also feel vulnerable. So the tendency is flight. It is simply a question of survival of the fittest. To fully understand the behavior in the *Lusitania*, researchers have suggested that the incident occurred during a major war, hence some of the passengers might have thought they were the target of an attack. However, the *Titanic* passengers exhibited "fight" syndrome. Therefore, the study concluded that the demonstration of flight-fight behavior in time of life-threatening situations is to a large degree determined by the time factor. This may suggest that victims will help others only when there is a little time to act or not act.

Even though the behavior of the passengers in the *Titanic* support the theory of potent instinct, I admit that our natural instinct is to some extent linked to and supported by socially constructed habits of particular societies, as the researchers cited above have attempted to show. What we are taught or observe from childhood naturally become part of our genetics and thus transferred from one generation to another.

Chapter 5

Emotional Influence on Policy Response

From the morning of September the 11th, 2001, to this hour, America
has been engaged in an unprecedented effort to defend our freedom
and our security ... With my signature, this act of Congress will
create a new Department of Homeland Security, ensuring that our
efforts to defend this country are comprehensive and united.
—George W. Bush, forty-third president of
the United States, November 2002

In this chapter, I identify and discuss a number of emergency-related
public policies and administrative decisions that have been triggered by
the aftermath of catastrophic events. The goal is to demonstrate how
emotions can drive policy decisions to mitigate and prepare for natural
and man-made tragedies. Evidence shows that whenever such events
occur, those charged with decisions capitalize on the emotionally charged
atmosphere to appeal for concrete policies, regulations, and formal
processes to reduce (or even prevent) such incidents from occurring in
the future. Generally, such decisions can be viewed as reactive rather
than proactive.

First, I go through relevant definitions and then review selected
studies that have attempted to show how emotions, particularly negative

emotions, have the tendency to influence human judgment and our choice of policy options. The aim is to demonstrate the extent to which negative emotions such as anger and sadness will push decision makers to propose, modify, enact, and implement policies aimed at reducing natural and man-made emergencies. As noted in chapter 1, other emotions such as empathy can lead to altruistic behaviors and actions by policy makers.

I argue in the second section of this chapter that, while evidence overwhelmingly supports the formalization of relevant policies, regulations, institutions, and processes primarily after an incident occurs, human rationality should drive these actors to be more proactive by planning, preparing, and mitigating all forms of emergencies. I further maintain that emergencies have the tendency to push us out of our self-interest zones to that of societal welfare in which we attempt to take actions that provide the greatest good for the greatest number. Interventions in emergencies make us recognize the necessity of human survival, whether next door or in distant lands. We are, so to speak, defenders of Homo sapiens' DNA from extinction.

Concepts and Previous Studies

Merriam-Webster Dictionary online defines emotion as "a conscious mental reaction (as anger or fear) subjectively experienced as strong feeling usually directed toward a specific object and typically accompanied by psychological and behavioral changes in the body." *Cambridge Dictionary* online defines the term simply as strong feelings such as love, anger, fear, etcetera. Another definition I find to be more apt is "a natural instinctive state of mind deriving from one's circumstances, mood, or relationships with others." Georges, Wiener, and Keller (2013) describe emotion as "any of the feelings of joy, sorrow, fear, hate, anger, love, etc." (p. 160). It is, therefore, an intense positive or negative feeling directed at someone or something. In this sense, there is a semblance between emotion and empathy.

Emotions can generally be categorized into positive emotion and negative emotion. The former includes feelings of joy, happiness, pride, love, empathy, hope, and surprise. The latter includes anger, sorrow, sadness, fear, hate, contempt, disgust, guilt, shame, frustration, and disappointment. Incidental emotion, another category that is relevant to understand how emotions influence our decisions, will be explored later in the chapter. This is a type of emotion that we tend to carry with us to the decision-making table even though it has no relevance to the issue being discussed and decided upon (Learner and Keltner, 2000). It is like a boss who had a bad experience before coming to work and exhibits those emotions in his communication with colleagues in the office. Some studies discuss the two elements of incidental emotion, anger and sadness/empathy, by suggesting that these attributes have the tendency to direct perceptions about the course of an event in opposite directions. For example, incidental anger focuses on internal attribution. In other words, specific individuals are assumed to be responsible for undesirable events and must be punished. On the other hand, incidental sadness points to external attribution, which means that the event owes its occurrence to the situation or circumstance (Learner and Keltner, 2000, p. 477).

In a case study of how the anger of the jurors influenced judgment on first-degree murder, Weiner and Keller (2013) found that the different levels of emotions resulting from testimonies in the court and their feelings for the victims and families shaped their final judgment to either sanction a life sentence or the death penalty. Although the jurors followed the instructions to consider the facts and evidence provided, emotions seemed to have influenced how they interpreted each piece of evidence provided and of course during their deliberations. Using the cognitive appraisal framework to measure the changes in emotions after testimony was provided, the authors sought to answer three primary questions: "What are the different types of positive and negative emotions the jurors feel? How do those emotions change over the course of the trial as the evidence unfolds? What is the relationship between the emotional reactions to evidence and judgment outcome?" (p. 156). One major finding of the study was that anger is the single most significant factor that influences judgment. The reason why anger dominates is because of its unique attributes. It has the ability to speedily grab attention, and it enables us to point at the individual responsible for the harmful incident. Surprisingly, the jurors did not seem to focus on the situation. It is for this reason, the investigators concluded, the angry jurors either sanctioned death penalty or life sentence.

Another study conducted by Learner and Keltner (2000) that aimed to determine how emotion influenced judgment and choice of action concluded that "momentary emotion" (i.e., reactions to a specific object) and "dispositional emotion" (i.e., a composite of anger and fear that directs emotion across time and situation) largely influence the nature of decisions (p. 477). The investigators further determined that emotions tend to take this important role because emotions attract quick responses on how to deal with an incident, and also, emotion "directs attention, memory, memory and judgment to address the emotion-eliciting event" (p. 476).

In a separate study by Sadler, Lineberger, Correll, and Park (2005) that assessed the links between emotion, attributions, and policy endorsement in response to the September 11 terrorist attacks, the results were no different. In fact, they confirmed the results of earlier studies conducted on the same subject. The only difference is that they expanded the list of measurable elements to include "attribution" (probable cause), "personal reaction," and "individual differences" of the study participants. The goal was to determine the degree to which incident and emotions experienced predicted the policy response to the event and any occurrence. The results showed that: a) anger caused the participants to attribute the incident to terrorism from extreme Islamism, hence an aggressive military response was preferred by the participants and overruled any form of humanitarian response; b) those who felt sad and fearful attributed the incident to lapses in security among other unknown factors, thus suggesting slow but calculated actions that address the circumstances leading to the attack; c) policy or any variance thereof is a function of attributions and emotions. In summary, the aggressive military policy response that used American forces to search for Osama Bin Laden in Afghanistan and his accomplices demonstrates the extent to which momentary and dispositional emotions were instrumental to the subsequent strategy for tackling terrorism.

Two other studies that confirm the efficacy of emotions in decision making include that of Aditi Mankad (2012) and Deborah Small and Jennifer Lerner (2008). Mankad conducted a study to determine how emotions influence decision making on decentralized water systems. In fact, by applying the functional approach, he established that emotions: a) provide information that can be used to appraise alternative options, b) enhance the speed and the seizing of opportunity for decision making, c) improve assessment of the situation; d) strengthen commitment of personal resources, and e) increase the ability to interpret risks because past emotional experiences are often retrieved to improve how the future is to be handled (p. 132–133).

Small and Lerner (2008) established that incidental anger and sadness shaped policy preferences for welfare recipients. They compared the characteristics of decision makers (political conservatives and political liberals), perceived characteristics of potential welfare recipients, and transient influences on policy preferences to see if there is a change in policy preferences among welfare recipients. The link between the attributions (cause of their needs) and how they were perceived (lazy or victims of circumstance) showed that overall: a) the perceptions about the degree of need (including sympathy) will determine the type of policy adopted; b) incidental anger, sadness, or sympathy toward this population characteristic will determine the readiness to extend assistance and therefore shape policy preference; and c) causes outside of one's control (i.e., external attributions) could indicate high levels of compassion (p. 150–160).

The results of these studies, as discussed in the following cases, attempt to elucidate why and how emotions (negative or positive) have shaped policy choices following the occurrence of black swan events (i.e., abrupt and unforeseen events such as mass murders by lunatics, earthquakes, hurricanes, plane, train and automobile crashes, and other similar emergencies).

Emotions and Policy Response to Emergencies: Some Examples

1. *Removal of the Confederate Flag, South Carolina—2015*

At the time of writing this section (June 28, 2015), the debate rages on among members of the public and specifically by the legislature in South Carolina's state capitol in Charleston. The debate is about the removal of the 154-year-old Confederate flag. The emotionally charged proposal was in response to the murder of nine African American parishioners by a twenty-one-year-old white supremacist, Dylann Roof, on June 17. Roof walked into the church during a Bible study conducted by Pastor Clemente Pinkney, who was also one of the state's senators to the local assembly. He reportedly received a warm welcome and sat there calmly for about an hour before he removed a .45-caliber Glock handgun and shot nine men and women who were in a Bible study. He was later apprehended as he tried to escape in the neighboring state of North Carolina.

The massacre immediately attracted a call for the removal of the Confederate battle flag currently hoisted on the state capitol rotunda. To many across the nation, the flag stood as a symbol of a racist past when the South engaged the North in a civil war (April 12, 1861–April 9, 1865) to keep slavery a legal institution, while the North wanted it banned. It is important to acknowledge here that there were other complex causes to the war. Generally, historians tend to trace the actual trigger of the war to the election of President Abraham Lincoln on March 4, 1861. He subsequently declared the Emancipation Declaration that essentially abolished slavery in the union. However, the South (Georgia, Florida, Mississippi, Alabama, Texas, Louisiana, Virginia, Arkansas, South Carolina, North Carolina, and Tennessee) refused to abide by the law and decided to secede by forming a separate nation, the Confederate States of America (HistoryNet.com). Some historians have contended that the proclamation only abolished slavery in the South while the Northern states were allowed to keep their slaves. If there is any truth in this, then it may have justified the Southerners' course to keep up the fight. It is also important to recognize that conflicts of interest on other issues were also determinants of the war. For example, the Southerners rallied against the power of national government. Instead, they preferred diffused power structures that could allow states to determine their own policies and destinies. The Northerners, on the other hand, were fearful of the stability of American democracy if the nation were to be divided into two major political factions.

Given that "a house divided cannot stand," Lincoln and his fellow Northerners engaged the South in a fierce battle to keep the nation from falling apart. Interestingly, the war started in Charleston, South Carolina, when the Southern Army declared Fort Sumter, a Union fort based in the harbor of Charleston, part of the Confederacy, by bringing down the Union flag down and hoisting their own. The war then erupted on a bigger scale and lasted for four years, with the South being defeated. The North had won because of its military might and larger population: 22 million versus 9.5 million to the south, of which 3.5 million were slaves. Some of the slaves escaped to join the Northern forces in their fight to end slavery and to save the union.

Even after the war ended, and into the twenty-first century, seven Southern states (Mississippi, Alabama, Arkansas, Florida, Georgia, North Carolina, and Tennessee) have kept this symbolically segregationist flag of the Confederacy flying high at the state capitol alongside the official US flag. I must, however, point out that not all white Americans in the South saw the flag as negatively. Meanwhile, a number of major highways, streets, and buildings continue to bear the names of Southern war heroes while the contested flag is issued on state license plates. Souvenirs that celebrate the Confederacy are commonplace in supermarkets, including megastores such as Wal-Mart and other online outlets. Such items certainly have no bounds in a free-market economy of today. However, when such symbolic items touch on the nerves of individual rights or remind a group of a racist past, then they can be questioned at the altar of policy bodies and institutions.

As a new battle erupted in South Carolina to get rid of the Confederate flag on state capital grounds, other states such as Mississippi began to revisit the preeminence of their own Confederate flags at certain sites. What gave this battle a national limelight is national statistics on African Americans living in the south where the contested flag prevails. Consider the following: In the 2010 census, the nation's one-third of African Americans (or twelve million) lived in the south where the remaining forty-eight million were categorized as Caucasian and other nonwhite populations. This means that the one-third black population is living under a state flag that evokes, if you will, a system that legitimized slave ownership (Ingraham, 2015).

When Dylann Roof shot the nine black Americans during a Bible study, investigators began to focus on the presence of the flag, as well as other personal items, in Roof's room. His car license plates also had the controversial flag, in addition to racist flags of Southern Rhodesia (now Zimbabwe) and South Africa under Apartheid on the T-shirt that he was wearing while brandishing a handgun. The photo helped investigators to understand his past and to determine a possible motive for the massacre.

Now the big question is, should the South Carolina legislative assembly rule in the favor of the removal of the flag from the state capital or not? The state's Heritage Act requires that any alteration of the Confederacy and Civil War statues or any monuments must be approved by two-thirds of the assembly votes. It is under this legal mandate that South Carolina's current legislature must work to determine what policy action they ought to take concerning the flag. Additionally, the policy actors must justify any connection between the flag as a symbol with the assailant's action. Similarly, they must examine the intended and unintended consequence of any decision. For example, will failure to remove the flag increase or not increase racial tensions? They must further contend with the dissenting view that the flag is simply a symbol of southern culture. Moreover, the decision makers must also consider the right of the state to display the flag as a form of free speech as provided by the First Amendment.

But let's stay focused on the thesis of this chapter that emotions caused by emergencies tend to propel policy actions to mitigate and prepare for such disasters from recurring. Let me recite the emotional overtones that were reported the day after the massacre and how they have shaped the policy debate within South Carolina's legislative assembly. Beginning with Ms. Hunter's online petition for the flag's removal that attracted 566,000 people within days, state Governor Nikki Haley, a Republican, was firm in her call for the same. Similar support came from unlikely quarters with Republican Paul Thurmond, a state senator, yielding to the demand and adding that his mind had been changed inside a church. As

New York Times reporters Michael Barbaro and Jonathan Martin (2015) stated, "a few days after the massacre, there seemed to be almost no one willing to speak up for the flag." It is apparent the legislators were pushed by emotional pressure to agree to the proposal for the flag removal that for many years was considered a symbol of southern heritage and pride. A moving speech by President Obama at the memorial service for the slain black pastor and state Senator Clemente Pinckney equally appealed to the emotions of those who were in a position of power to do something about the flag that reminded black people of the heinous past of slavery. His words are worth quoting:

> For too long we were blind to the pain that the Confederate flag stirred in too many of our citizens. It is true, a flag did not cause these murders. But as people from all walks of life, Republicans and Democrats, now acknowledge—including Governor Haley, whose recent eloquence on the subject is worthy of praise—as we all have to acknowledge, the flag has always represented more than just ancestral pride. (Shear, 2015)

Soon after the incident and the ensuing moving speeches, state governors of Georgia, Tennessee, and Virginia opted to halt the issuing of specialty license plates that featured the Confederate flag. As Mississippi pondered what to do, Alabama Governor Robert Bentley ordered the immediate removal of four such flags from a monument at the state capitol grounds (Bradner, 2015). What is also interesting is the decision by Wal-Mart Stores and Amazon to remove confederate-themed items from their shelves (Borden and Berman, 2015).

The first week of July saw the bill to remove the flag from the capitol ground passed in the Senate with 37–3 vote. The same bill was thereafter passed by the House of Representatives with 94–20 vote, after a gruesome debate that went close to midnight. Upon the final vote, state Governor Nikki Haley commented, "No one should drive by the statehouse and feel like they don't belong." She further added that the compassion demonstrated by the relatives of the victims helped lead the state legislators to pass the bill with an overwhelming majority. In fact, the bill was passed despite the proposed twenty-five amendments that were rejected outright by the majority of legislatures (Payne and Ford, 2015; Self, 2015). To send a strong symbolic message to all, the governor signed the bill on Thursday, July 9 (2015) with nine different pens. Each pen was to be delivered to the families of the nine church victims.

The following day, Friday, July 10, at exactly 10:00 a.m., a ceremony featured live on CNN began in front of the state capitol where the flag had flown high each day since 1961. A large crowd stood by and chanted, "USA, USA," as members of South Carolina's Highway Patrol Honor Guard removed the historic flag. Its permanent resting place is the Confederate Relic Room and Military Museum.

> Although the actual rolling down of the flag took about two minutes, the process started, as we now know, with the shooting of nine Black parishioners by White supremacist Dylann Roof. Then emotions spiked as pictures showed the shooter posing next to the Confederate flag. As the message to remove the flag went viral across the nation, the governor and state legislators delved deeper into the debate to bring the flag down. There is no doubt, at least in my mind, that this particular case strengthens the assertion that emotions arising out of emergencies can indeed trigger the adoption of relevant, but reactive policies. In fact, this apparent relationship between emotions and legislative actions is best reflected in Governor Haley's statement upon signing the bill:

> "This is a story about how the action of nine individuals laid out this long chain of events that forever showed the state of South Carolina what love and forgiveness look like ... This compassion helped lead to the legislature to send her the bill allowing for the flag to be taken down." (Barman, 2015)

It is also noteworthy that positions on the flag debate were changed by the nature of the murders and the ensuing emotional speeches and blog posts that came from every corner of the nation. Particularly noticeable was the governor's change of position and the subsequent call for action that bookended the historic debate over the South's iconic but disgraceful symbol. The governor's emotions probably deepened over the issue after attending the funerals of all the nine victims.

Generally, experience does show that policies arising out of black swan events can have cascading effects. Consider the following: Soon after the historic passage of South Carolina's legislation, US Congress House Speaker John Boehner called for a review of the display of Confederacy symbols and memorabilia on federal property, such as national cemeteries where Confederate soldiers are buried. Unfortunately, with the notoriety of gridlocks for which the US Congress is known, it is unlikely that such a proposal will be tackled swiftly as in South Carolina. Another change of position (or in policy) after the legislation was the declaration by the National Collegiate Athletic Association (NCAA) to lift a fifteen-year ban that prevented the state from hosting championship games. Additionally, the National Association for the Advancement of Colored People (NAACP) has responded by rescinding its persistent call for travel boycotts and tourism of the state (Kane and Phillip, 2015). The timing of these policy decisions, we can safely argue, has been largely determined by tragic incidents or what policy experts call "focus events," which tend to be abrupt and have widespread effects.

Although I relied on press reports for many of the facts discussed above, I once asked a friend and policy expert, Richard Huff, with whom I have worked for years, what he thought about the entire saga. This is what he had to say:

> It does divert attention from the gun control issue in this crime. I think the flag should not be part of a government function (on state houses, license plates or other) or used as an official symbol because of its history. It represents treason and implies hatred. It offends, much like the Nazi flag would. For private display, that is another thing. But

one common thread of most major crimes involve mass shootings. Whether the shooter has obtained the gun legally or not is a smoke screen. I don't have a criminal or mental illness history, but we should not be allowed to own an automatic weapon period. They are for the military, not even law enforcement. Until this changes, we'll continue to have these tragedies. I don't see it changing at all. (Richard Huff, personal communication, July 10, 2015)

Huff raises three important issues worthy of consideration: Should the flag be a government function (on state houses, license plates, or other)? Should a flag be used as an official symbol because of its history? Should citizens, other than those in the military and the police force, own guns? With the recent increase in police shootings of unarmed citizens in the United States, concern is emerging as to whether these law enforcement street-level bureaucrats should actually be permitted to own guns. It is my view that if America is to effectively address the issue of mass murders, gun control must be examined more boldly, including the possibility of re-amending the Second Amendment to the Constitution that legalizes gun ownership by whoever is interested.

In the next section, I explore a case in which US Congress attempted to address the subject of gun control following a mass murder but failed because of pro-gun factions who filibustered the bill before it could gain ground beyond the precincts of Capitol Hill.

2. *Congress Debates Manchin-Toomey Bill (Sandy Hook Murder)—2013*

At the memorial church service for the twenty slain elementary school children and their six teachers in Newton, Connecticut, that occurred on December 14, 2012, President Obama sounded these emotional words:

We've endured too many of these tragedies in the past few years. And each time I learn the news, I react not as a president, but as anybody else would as a parent. And that was especially true today. I know there's not a parent in America who doesn't feel the same overwhelming grief that I do. As a country, we have been through this too many times. Whether it is an elementary school in Newtown, or a shopping mall in Oregon, or a temple in Wisconsin, or a movie theater in Aurora, or a street corner in Chicago, these neighborhoods are our neighborhoods and these children are our children. And we're going to have to come together and take meaningful action to prevent more tragedies like this, regardless of the politics.

As these words echoed the nation's experience with unabated murders in every major city and county each week, a number of people called for stiffer gun control laws immediately following the massacre by twenty-year-old Adam Lanza. Although the right to own guns is embedded in the Second Amendment to the US Constitution, supporters of gun control believe the system of gun acquisition is presently less strict in a number of states and stricter in select few. Nonetheless, following the brutal murder of the children, the need to control who can obtain guns was pushed up the agenda in the national debate. That prompted Senator Pat Toomey (Republican, Pennsylvania) and Senator Joe Manchin (Democrat, West Virginia) to introduce a bill (i.e., Manchin-Toomey Bill) in Congress that would make it much harder for individuals to acquire guns at will. Specifically, the bill aimed to expand existing background checks to those who buy guns on the Internet and at gun shows, and by those who have a record of mental sickness. Accordingly, the bill sought to: 1) make it a federal crime to buy a gun and then give it to someone whom the buyer has "reasonable cause" to believe is prohibited from having one; 2) have states develop a list of prohibited purchases into a national database. At this time in history, background checks are only required for those who buy at federally licensed gun dealers (Plumer, 2013). Despite its timeliness and importance, the bill was defeated in the Senate with a 54–46 vote; sixty votes were needed to move it to the next stage. In reaction, President Obama blamed the insensitivity of those who failed to support what he called "the common-sense gun reforms" even as the bereaved families watched the voting process from the Senate gallery. He added:

> Families that know unspeakable grief summoned the courage to petition their elected leaders—not just to honor the memory of their children, but to protect the lives of all our children. And a few minutes ago, a minority in the United States Senate decided it wasn't worth it ... Sooner or later, we are going to get this right. The memories of these children demand it. And so do the American people. (*Time* staff, 2013)

3. *USA Patriot Act and Homeland Security Act*

Considered one of the most historic and important pieces of legislation (or amendments) in recent US history was the swift passage of the Uniting and Strengthening America by Providing Appropriate Tools Required to Intercept and Obstruct Terrorism Act (USA Patriot Act). Passed by US Congress and signed into law on October 26, 2001, by President George W. Bush, just forty-five days after 9/11, the act was both a rational and emotional reaction to the terrorist attack that caused 2,973 deaths (9/11 Commission Report).

The primary aim of the act was to discourage any future terrorist attacks by enhancing investigatory tools and to prosecute those involved in money laundering because it could potentially open doors to funding terrorists. It is this legislation that authorized wiretapping telephone conversations of citizens as well as the search of e-mail communications and other private records, including storage of personal information in massive data centers or servers. Most of the provisions were meant to expire by 2006 but were reauthorized by Congress on March 1 of the same year (Library of Congress, 2015).

To make the Patriot Act a permanent feature that can deal with the rising global terrorist threats, the previously existing Hart-Rudman Commission was expanded together with elements of Patriot Act to create The Homeland Security Act (HSA) of 2002. The act was passed the same year on November 25 (Homeland Security, 2002). The act's objectives were to first consolidate over twenty federal agencies (e.g., Federal Emergency Management Agency, US Secret Service, US Customs Service, US Coast Guard, and Immigration and Naturalization Service) into a single agency—the Department of Homeland Security under a cabinet-level secretary. This and the Department of Defense are now the biggest federal departments.

As was previously mentioned at the beginning of this chapter, studies on 9/11 by Lineberger, Correll, and Park (2005), among others, have shown that anger caused those surveyed to attribute the incident to terrorism. Second, those who felt sad and fearful attributed the incident to lapses in security. The survey participants thus recommended deliberate approaches that would take into consideration the circumstances leading to the attack. Third, the authors concluded that a policy (such as the Patriot Act and the Homeland Security Act) or any variance thereof is a function of attributions and emotions. The quick passage of the two acts by Congress and the subsequent establishment of one of the biggest government bureaucracies in US history demonstrate the extent to which momentary and dispositional emotions (or potent instinct) can actually influence the timing of public policy and administrative decisions to mitigate, prepare for, and respond to catastrophic events.

4. *Establishment of Environment Protection Act after the Bhopal Disaster*

Two years after Union Carbide's pesticide plant in Bhopal, India, killed 3,800 people and caused the increased morbidity and premature deaths of about 15,000–20,000 in the subsequent two decades, the government of India responded to citizens' anger by passing the Environment and Protection Act in 1986. The act led to the creation of a new bureaucracy, the Ministry of Environment and Forests, whose purpose is to coordinate the activities of several regulatory agencies and to create rules and procedures that prevent environmental hazards to human safety and health. Another reaction through which the affected citizens expressed their negative emotions was litigation. A number of court cases were launched that demanded compensation from the Union Carbide Corporation and the government of India that held 22 percent of the shares through a subsidiary, Union Carbide India Limited. A total of USD $470 million was awarded to the complainants. To ensure that compensation was equitable, the government of India enacted the Bhopal Gas Leak Act.

On the part of Union Carbide head office in the United States, the incident led to a number of policy and administrative actions. First, the corporation quickly closed down its facility in West Virginia for further inspection and to avoid a similar catastrophe from occurring. Second, at the national level, the Bhopal tragedy motivated legislators to reauthorize the Environmental Protection Agency's Federal Superfund, which helped bring about a network of local emergency planning councils to deal with safety issues and similar disasters in the future. Additionally, the Bhopal incident caused the Chemical Manufacturers Association to establish a Community Action Emergency Response (CAER) organization, whose primary goal was to prevent and respond to industrial emergencies (Browning, 1983).

5.   *1986—Civil Protection Committee Created, Mexico*

Months after the September 1985 earthquake that killed over 10,000 people in Mexico City, emotions across the country triggered the creation of Civil Protection Committee (CPC). This also followed the death of one hundred volunteers who managed to rescue eight hundred victims. The government quickly endorsed CPC as one of the emergency response institutions whose role is to protect, educate, and respond to disasters such as earthquakes and tsunamis. The committee has expanded its personnel and trained to lead in drills and other emergency preparedness and awareness activities. In addition to expanding their branches across the country, they have also been able to participate in international rescue operations in Haiti, El Salvador, and Taiwan after they were hit by earthquakes and tsunamis (Enders, 2010; FEMA, 2015).

6. *1999—United Nations Office for Disaster Risk Reduction Established*

As early as 1965, the United Nations General Assembly had begun to recognize the growing plight of nations in which deaths and destruction and property were increasingly becoming frequent. For example, after the deaths of over 13,000 from the Buyin-Zara (Iran) and Skopje (Macedonia/Yugoslavia) earthquakes, the General Assembly adopted in 1965 Resolution #1882 to require states to provide financial assistance to victims of natural disasters (U.N.org, 2015). That initiative was again expanded in 1970 with Resolution #2717. This time, the secretary-general was required to institute pre-disaster planning at domestic and international levels, and to integrate research and technology to mitigate widespread casualties from natural disasters. Despite these earlier attempts, representatives at the UN again in 1971 adopted Resolution #2816 to formally create the United Nations Disaster Relief Office (UNDRO). The purpose of UNDRO was to advise governments on pre-disaster planning (UNISDR.Org).

The United Nations further demonstrated its commitment to responding to these disasters by declaring the 1990s as the "The International Decade for Natural Disaster Reduction," that included inter alia the preparation of a framework for action. Another resolution (#48/188) was passed to convene a world conference on disaster reduction. These combined efforts, from the 1960s to the end of 2007, ended up with the adoption of thirty-six resolutions by the UN General Assembly. The timing of the resolutions was, for the most part, occasioned by increased number of disasters, loss of human lives, and destruction of infrastructure.

Chapter 6

Incorporating Ordinary Citizens

Since all citizens are likely to be affected by emergency
management policies ... They should be integrated into the
early stages of response and recovery.
—Federal Emergency Management Agency

This chapter is divided into four sections. The first section presents
a broad rationale for training and why it is important for ordinary
bystanders to possess basic skills that can be used to rescue those in life-
threatening situations. The following section examines different types
of training or approaches that are generally applied by different agencies
to improve the emergency response skills of nonprofessionals. The third
section presents a number of real incidents in which bystanders with
relevant emergency response skills have successfully applied those skills
to save lives. In the fourth section, examples of where a lack of training
has either restrained rescue or caused harm to the rescuer are included.

Rationale for Bystander Training

Generally, emergency preparedness, mitigation, and rescue operations
are functions of government institutions and specialized agencies on the
local, national, and international levels, such as the Red Cross, the Red

Crescent, and Doctors without Borders (*Médicins Sans Frontierès*). Some governments that recognize the importance of this societal welfare role dedicate substantial amounts of funds to support emergency institutions. However, while such institutions and funds do play an important role, the capacity of those who provide emergency services is just as important. Additionally, what we see in practice is that governments and nongovernmental agencies tasked with these functions have unknowingly developed the ideology of reactive response to emergencies. Over the past decade, however, and particularly after the 9/11 incident, US federal agencies and the Department of Homeland Security, for example, have reversed that ideology to a proactive approach. What we see today is an intensified training program within national agencies and at the local levels. In fact, community emergency response teams (CERT) have emerged in at least twenty-eight states across the United States as a result of this shift in training policy. This, however, does not preclude the operations of professional rescuers who are—to a large degree— quite efficient in most cities and states. FEMA has further acknowledged that emergency crews cannot always reach incident locations the same minute they occur. Traffic, communication failures, and the number of victims involved can often overwhelm the capacity of professional rescuers even if they reach the scene in two to five minutes. This is true in major disasters such hurricanes, tornadoes, earthquakes, tsunamis, floods, and train crashes, among others. This is why bystanders can be relied upon to assist, especially when they have the necessary skills.

As illustrated by the response to the 9/11 tragedy, most of those who were self-dispatched did so out of instincts and altruism despite their lack of training in first aid or incident command ("Basic Concepts," 2010). The results of their intervention were both positive and negative. One positive result, for example, was providing material support such as food, blankets, and other supplies that were needed. The negative was the added confusion created by their presence as each volunteer, without guidance, did whatever he or she thought was logical in order to rescue victims trapped under the huge pile of debris. In fact, some of the bystanders were killed in the process. Unfortunately, after a brief time following the incident, professional rescuers found the presence of volunteers a problem in itself; valuable time was spent managing them instead of the disaster. At the Pentagon crash site, military volunteers decided to help by running in and out of the burning building. Some were able to rescue victims, but several of the volunteers sustained injuries because they did not have the appropriate gear or training. As the above-cited source has shown, when bystanders ran to the scene of an emergency to rescue victims, they often created more chaos than order. In fact, there is no accountability or determination of who is in charge of first aid, removal of the injured, or transportation of the victims to the nearest medical facility. Lessons learned from lay responders to the 9/11 incident and other similar cases call for acknowledging the "limitations, training discrepancies, lack of standardized training and accreditation or certification, and terminology differences faced within the response communities" ("Basic Concepts," 2010, p. 2). This statement about the need for training coincides with the 2012 findings of a survey I conducted in the United Arab Emirates and Kenya.

Another argument for the support of bystander first-responder training is that rescuing an emergency victim is not as simple as it may appear. It can be physically challenging (especially when equipment is required but unavailable) and stressful. Moreover, bystanders who respond to emergencies must not only be able to provide the help they set out to do, but they must also be able to protect themselves from personal harm. There are a number of cases where well-intentioned bystanders lost their lives in the process of saving others but were also unable to save the victim in the first plan, a double tragedy. Today, with the increased use of smartphones, bystanders are usually the first to call for emergency services, and whenever possible, they may move in to rescue victims. It therefore makes sense for these nonprofessional first responders to possess some basic skills that they can employ to help those in critical conditions. Examples might include saving a choking or drowning child.

Other attributes that often skip our minds are courage and the willingness to intervene in emergencies. While others might argue that these two attributes are innately unique to selected individuals, I contend that training can, in fact, prepare, unlock, and strengthen the potential in each of us. In particular, the willingness to assist an injured person or a cardiac arrest victim is primarily motivated by the relevant skills possessed by the bystander. In such incidents, those without any relevant skills will be reluctant to intervene. Rather, they will call out for anyone else with appropriate skills to come and assist.

Skill-Based Training Approaches

1. Mandated and Certified Training

One of the most effective approaches is for governments to mandate standardized and certified training on emergency preparedness and response. In order to provide effective training, it is important for government agencies to be provided with the financial resources, tools, and equipment that they need. This is exactly what the US government has done by creating Federal Emergency Management Agency (FEMA). FEMA has further supported the creation of community emergency response teams (CERTs) in at least twenty-eight states. Another agency, National Incident Management System (NIMS), was similarly created to train first responders ("Basic Concepts," 2010). A number of European governments have continued to support similar efforts by passing laws and availing resources to facilitate training in emergency response.

Institutional-Based Training

In their book *Why Nations Fail*, Daron Acemoglu and James Robinson (2012) provide a more convincing narrative of why public institutions are instrumental to economic development. Institutions, they suggest, are the foundation of society's success. They are capable of organizing societal resources that can be used to mitigate and respond to different types of emergencies.

Institutions, broadly defined, are not just departments or established agencies to provide services but can also be conceived as rules, procedures, and systems that guide organized groups or agencies to achieve their strategic goals. This perspective is no different when thinking about emergencies and how to respond. FEMA, NIMS, the Red Cross, the Red Crescent, Doctors without Borders, Homeland Security (specialized agencies), St. John Ambulance, city/municipal firefighters, and the police are classic examples of emergency institutions that are making a difference between life and death. The mechanisms employed by these agencies, particularly those employed after the 9/11 incident, include face-to-face and/or online emergency awareness training, regular drills, and exercises.

This, of course, can be linked to emergencies and how we ought to prepare and respond to them through education and debates about their causes and solutions. While I don't intend to engage the reader in an intellectual treatise, I wish to go back to the ancient Greeks about the importance of education (or training). Plato, an eminent Greek philosopher, believed that an ideal city (read: republic, nation, city, municipality) required ideal education in music, mathematics, gymnastics, and dialectics. The goal of including these elements was to satisfy three desires of our souls: the appetitive (pleasure), the spirited (honor), and the rational (knowledge). As Aristotle later acknowledged, the acquisition of all the above served as a prerequisite to the ultimate human potential, the ability to engage in dialectics. In Aristotle's view, dialectics was the rational stage of our abilities to engage in questioning and answering some of the toughest issues faced by humankind. It is, I would argue, the type of intellect that unlocks the human potential to solve problems that confront humanity day in and out. Thus, as rational beings, and by acquiring training that prepares us to mitigate and respond to random or predicted natural hazards, we will have satisfied the rational part of our being that Plato enunciated in his writings.

Dialectics can thus help us understand what to do with harmful events that have the tendency to overwhelm our physical capacity and intellects. It is this spirit that Robert Sapien and Andrew Allen (2001) endorse the idea of institutionalizing emergency training to school children. With this kind of early preparation, emergency preparedness becomes a part of their rational being and subsequently their societal culture. Greek philosopher Aristotle once opined that this kind of education opens up the opportunity for continued dialectics or debates about societal welfare, especially in city-states.

Sapien and Allen add that it would be a worthwhile project to begin educating children early if we hope to curb the number of humans that are subjected to the wrath of black swan events. Children, for example, spend about 28 percent of their day (or 14 percent of their total yearly hours) in school (p. 329). The question that they raise is: are the institutions and/or the children prepared to face emergencies that often arise unannounced? To prove the gravity of this concern, the study shows that some 600,000 children in the United States are rushed to the hospital for unexpected injuries while at school, and about sixteen million children are treated in emergency departments annually for the same type of incidental injuries (p. 329). The purpose of the study was to try to assess the degree to which school nurse training was linked to student injuries or lack thereof. Interestingly, the findings did prove that the number of student injuries increased particularly in environments where in-house nurses lacked, or had only minimal, relevant training in emergency preparedness and response. It is in response to this training need that the American College of Emergency Physicians School of Health Task Force was formed.

2. Integrating Emergency Training in School Curriculum

The idea of training students in schools as a captive audience can make a huge difference in society and how we respond to emergencies. Several reasons justify this option. One, students are generally energetic and eager to learn. Therefore, it would be worthwhile not just to conduct emergency drills and exercises but also to integrate elements of emergency mitigation, preparedness, and response strategies into course curriculum. This could start at the elementary level and continue through university. If you can recall the shooting of twenty children and six teachers at Sandy Hook Elementary School in Newton, Connecticut, the manner in which the teachers handled the situation was commendable. Some guided their students to safer rooms, and all the little ones followed. Had they not had any basic emergency training and awareness, the number of casualties may have been much greater.

Another reason why emergency training needs to be more focused and intensified in schools is to identify capable individuals who can then train others (the training of trainers). A number of studies do show that peer-to-peer learning is highly effective because there is a connection in addition to the fact that peers do listen to each other. This might be contentious in other societies. In my own Western Kenya culture, younger people by tradition and practice tend to listen to the advice from their seniors and are likely to take for granted the advice by their peers. However, in a study that examined the effects of the training of trainers in school-based intervention in first aid and risk reduction, Carutth et al. (2010) confirmed that this model of training, especially among high school students, improved self-assurance from lack of confidence, reciprocal information exchange, transference of risk reduction, and generational synergy ("pulling together as a team") (p. 458). This is because peer-to-peer information sharing is apparently more effective.

It is also conceivable that schools are a better place to inculcate the culture of emergency preparedness among the young. Schools are also where their cognitive capabilities are developed. What they are taught in school is likely to last in their brains over the course of their lives.

Collaborative Community-Based Training

In order to address the effects of widespread emergencies, countries that are well endowed with resources and human capacity have recognized that much more can be achieved through collaboration. Designated government agencies charged with emergency planning and response find it beneficial to collaborate with affected communities and other interested parties. The main goal of such collaboration is to tap synergy and to provide hard-to-reach communities with the skills and knowledge they will need whenever natural and man-made disasters occur. Foremost, it is critical for communities and individual citizens to be able to quickly recognize a real emergency, its size and its potential impact. Hence, training that covers the following four areas is appropriate and could be beneficial to ordinary citizens: fire safety, light search (i.e. being able to provide preliminary search of a building or to locate victims with minor or no injuries and help them exit from lightly damaged buildings; secondary searches are generally the role of experts with proper equipment), team organization, and disaster medical operation (Federal Emergency Management Agency, 2015). Of course, ordinary citizens are not expected to be as knowledgeable or to possess the ultimate skills as professionals in an emergency, but collaborative training would better prepare them to handle such situations to minimize casualties before professionals arrive.

Take for example the twelve tribes in the state of Arizona that have for a long time experienced floods from the Colorado River, wildfires, and infectious disease outbreaks such as West Nile virus and avian influenza. In order to deal with these emergencies and to reduce their effects on humans and property, the tribal leaders arranged a collaborative training initiative with the University of Arizona and the Arizona Department of Health Services (Pate and Mullins, 2008). The primary purpose was to acquire the basic skills, knowledge, and abilities that would prepare them to respond to the kinds of emergencies to which their communities were regularly vulnerable. Through this collaboration, a number of training modules for tribal health care representatives were developed and implemented. Although limited resources constrained comprehensive success with the program, basic competencies in emergency response were achieved.

Another example of a successful community-based training program is the community emergency response teams initiated by the Los Angeles City Fire Department in 1985. Recognizing that major disasters, whenever they occur, will generally overwhelm the capacity of existing professional rescuers, the city fire department created the Disaster Preparedness Division. The more compelling rationales were that emergencies come unannounced, that emergencies are random, and that emergencies can be widespread in their effects. Moreover, professionals often face challenges in reaching the scenes of such incidents in a timely fashion. One reason is communication failures. In many cities around the world, there are no lanes dedicated to emergency vehicles. Even when the sirens are loudly sounded for other vehicles to give way, the frequent gridlocks in large cities will often slow down the rescue crew. This can have the unintended consequence of lives lost in the last minutes prior the rescuer arrival. Given these realities, the US Federal Emergency Management Agency (FEMA) adopted and expanded the Los Angeles model by creating the Emergency Management Institute (EMI) and National Fire Academy (Federal Emergency Management Agency, 2015). These initiatives led to the setting up of volunteer-based community emergency response teams (CERT) currently in twenty-eight states. As FEMA has rationalized through its support of CERTs in various communities, citizens should be trained in basic lifesaving skills like rescue safety, knowledge of what to expect in the aftermath of a major disaster, and individual or group responsibility for preventing and preparing for such incidents. Additionally, such training aims to equip them with emotional preparedness to assist victims before professional help arrives.

In order to set up a CERT and to follow through to its institutionalization and success, FEMA recommends following four major steps: starting, delivery, maintaining involvement, and availing resources. Full details of this process are available in appendix 2.

Further efforts by FEMA included the passage of Post-Katrina Emergency Management Reform Act (Curry 2011). The purpose was to institutionalize what they called "synergistic protection." Through these, citizens and business entities that possess emergency-related skills and equipment are encouraged to volunteer by registering into a community database their contact information.

The University of South Florida is another good example of an institute that has successfully collaborated with the community to promote coalitions for better emergency response training. In a systematic study conducted by Frahm et al. (2014), teams of participants were offered a two-year training to support coalition-building efforts in different regions of the state. The participants also attended online and refresher courses in addition to face-to-face exercises and team activities. Results from the 184 community participants who attended from thirty-one Florida counties showed increased knowledge scores in overall emergency preparedness, mitigation, response, and sustenance of disaster coalitions. The study further proved the importance of coalition-building efforts, especially in dealing with disasters. Specifically, it noted that coalitions can be cost saving when each group member contributes whatever they have toward the greater good. Moreover, coalitions enable group members to tap into shared decisions, different capabilities, information, and other unique attributes that can contribute to successful mitigation and response. Despite these potential benefits, building and sustaining coalitions can be challenging, especially when goals are not clearly defined. Similarly, diversity can be nerve-wracking when the leadership is weak or when everyone (or every group) has a different perspective on how to go about implementing mitigation and response strategies. Unless discipline is exercised, coordination can become a nightmare, thus defeating the purpose for which the emergency coalition was formed.

To mitigate these problems and to improve the effectiveness and overall sustenance of such efforts, Frahm et al. (2014) recommend community-based disaster coalition training. It is in this regard that the University of South Florida created its Preparedness and Emergency Learning Center (USF-PERLC) (p. 111). A follow-up study has confirmed that participants in that training have subsequently applied their training skills and have "become more proactive about partnering with other agencies" (p. 115).

3. Preparing Health Education Specialists

There is an increasing need to ready health education specialists to better prepare and to provide adequate support to colleagues in the workplace, schools, and various clients. In the how-to piece of their article, Geiger, Firsing III, Beric, and Rodger (2013) provide the following guide for whenever emergencies occur:

Preparing for Emergencies

    a. **Train and Prepare Yourself**: Review policies and procedures pertinent to your setting or organization.

    b. **Train and Prepare Others**: Free courses are available online (e.g., FEMA's http://ready.gov). If you have the authority, make it a requirement for employees or students to take the course. The Red Cross has similar free classes (See: http://www.redcross.org/ux/take-a-class).

    c. **Setting Specific Preparation**: Identify vulnerabilities in your setting; develop the capacity to prevent and respond to the location-specific emergencies; make plans for recovery and improvements.

d. **Assess the Crisis and Respond**: The rationale is to ensure the safety of those involved, assess the dynamics of the incident, and how to respond. It is at this stage that inventory is taken of those injured, missing, and who is to taken for immediate medical care, and of course calling for professional assistance. Try to locate first aid toolkits and other essentials.

e. **Recovering from Emergencies**: Provide support, counseling, and meetings with relatives and other affected stakeholders.

Ensuring Training Content Is Retained

Yes, training is critical to preparing for emergencies, but unless regular exercises and drills are conducted, the response to emergencies from ordinary citizens can be disappointing at times. In the case of a real fire, the panicky public is likely to forget the procedures and take on the heels through any exit available, including front doors and, worse, windows. In big cities where loud emergency sirens and drills are common, students (in the library, for example) or employees (in offices) can be reluctant at times to evacuate the building when in fact there is a real emergency. As I have personally observed, at least in a Middle Eastern country where I taught at a university for three years, people are so used to the sirens that they occasionally mistake the real emergency siren for a regular drill. This can be a fatal mistake. Despite these occasional mistakes, conducting disaster exercises and fire drills can save lives. The following paragraphs provide a review of some studies that support this view.

In a study to understand how disaster exercises can enhance effective emergency preparedness in the U.K., Hakkyong Kim (2014) first observed that exercises serve two important roles. First, they familiarize everyone with the standard procedures of how to respond when an emergency strikes. The second is that they are able to identify potential problems associated with communication and coordination. The second observation by Kim is that almost all emergencies require cooperation between professional crews and other nonprofessionals, and among all affected groups and agencies in the vicinity of the incident. It is only through this synergy that casualties can be minimized. The third observation is that the minimization of casualties lies not primarily on the response phase but in the preparation phase. This is where exercises, especially those involving a number of stakeholder agencies, are critical for a number of reasons. The exercise provides an opportunity to observe each other's approaches and procedures, sharing skills and boosting participants' confidence, bravery, and willingness to confront an emergency when it strikes. In essence, exercises are generally conducted to test, train, and validate (p. 850). This triage process (i.e., sorting victims to determine medical priority in order to increase the number of survivors) does help with establishing the appropriateness of existing response plans and procedures for evacuations and management of chemical disasters.

Despite the logical basis of testing, training, and validating procedures for emergency preparedness and response, in real emergencies where actions are constrained by time and resources, it seems acceptable to be adaptive. As the foregoing study in the U.K. discovered, first responders not only follow the routines as laid out on paper but for the most part adapt to the changing conditions. It is also important to recognize that successful outcome of exercises should involve ordinary citizen volunteers rather than limit them to members of specific fraternity, organization, or school. They can often provide useful recommendations on the entire process, including debriefing, because in real emergencies, citizens outside of one's organization will be at the incident scene and will be affected as well.

A separate empirical study by Perry (2004), while confirming the findings by Kim (2014) on the potential benefits of disaster exercises in promoting effective emergency management, adds that participation in regular drills actually enhances "the perceptions of response knowledge and teamwork" for police officers, firefighters, and civilian volunteers (p. 64). A second benefit is the opportunity that exercises provide for detecting difficulties associated with performing actual response per standard procedures. Third, exercises promote cooperation within departments and across organizations. This can improve the effectiveness of any emergency response and reduce casualties. Fourth, exercises can enhance public knowledge of existing plans, thus reducing fear while at the same time increasing overall compliance with the recommended procedures should an emergency occur that demands their participation. Fifth, such regular drills serve an educational function as they expose participants to the types of and use of equipment in the aftermath of an emergency.

A number of conclusions can be drawn from these studies: First, while institutions should have approved emergency plans and procedures that include exercises and drills to test protocols and equipment and to train and validate their efficacy (Kim, 2014), such plans should allow for flexibility and innovations in actual rescue operations. This is because circumstances do change, and at times the application of imagination can save the day. Second, exercises offer participants the chance to enhance and demonstrate their expected levels of knowledge, skills, and abilities to respond to real emergencies. Third, exercises highly improved the confidence of civilian volunteers much more than professional responders (i.e., police and firefighters) as a result of new knowledge and skills. They felt that they were better prepared and were more ready to confront emergencies. This improved confidence as a result of preparedness through training and exercises prove the main thesis of this chapter that training matters. Agencies ought to integrate ordinary citizens in emergency response not simply because there are always willing bystanders that do it for free but to provide them with basic lifesaving skills so that they can help reduce the number of casualties in the first critical moments of a disaster.

In the next section, I take this further to examine a few cases in which training has proved its case, allowing those who have the requisite skills to bravely and willingly respond to emergencies. Such bravery is often backed by prior knowledge and skills acquired through training, exposure, and exercises.

Relevance of Training

Consider the case of the 1985 Mexico City earthquake. In that incident, hundreds of ordinary volunteers, many of whom were untrained in emergency rescue operations, came out to provide assistance to the victims. Although the outcome was very positive because as many as eight hundred victims were rescued, one hundred of these volunteers lost their lives in the process. It has been argued by many, and especially by Federal Emergency Management Agency (FEMA), that such a loss is a high price to pay in the name of volunteering. Certainly, even though the instinct to rescue those faced by life-threatening situations is compelling, studies as well as interviews I conducted in 2012 strongly concur with the views of FEMA that training to provide basic lifesaving skills to willing citizens is indeed essential. Hence the question that FEMA has repeatedly asked: "What can government do to (better) prepare citizens for this eventuality? (i.e., bystander's loss of life in rescue attempts). I also attempt to show that training and competence can enhance a bystander's willingness to intervene. This is particularly true in areas such as medical emergencies, including cardiac arrest and other rare incidents such as a massive inferno, the implosion of a coal mine, or a nuclear disaster. Rescues in such incidents often demand technical skills and relevant prior training.

Terrorist Attack in High-Speed Train—France

On August 21, 2015, a twenty-five-year-old Moroccan terrorist named Ayoub El-Khazzani was ambushed by three brave men as he loaded his AK-47 assault rifle at the entrance of a bathroom on a high-speed service train from the Netherlands to the French capital of Paris. He also had a Lugar automatic pistol, with eight magazines of thirty bullets in each magazine, and a box cutter. As the moment the AK rifle appeared jammed, three brave passengers who were nearby jumped to tackle the man. First was Mark Moogalian, a fifty-one-year-old French American who encountered the gunman and tried to wrestle the rifle from him. Moogalian was shot in the neck. Fortunately, three other Americans who were vacationing in Europe—Anthony Sadler, Spencer Stone, and Alek Skarlatos, came to his aid. Stone was wounded in the head and neck but managed to assist Moogalian, whose throat had been cut, by applying pressure to the man's neck to help him avoid bleeding out. Stone and Skarlatos moved in and overpowered the assailant by holding on to his neck and grabbing the handgun. Skarlatos then took the AK and used it to hit the assailant's head repeatedly. At that point, everyone nearby started punching and beating the alleged terrorist as Stone continued to keep him in a chokehold until he went unconscious. They then tied him before releasing him to security at the next rail station of Arras in northern France.

It is evident that the actions taken by these brave men, particularly the manner in which they tackled the terrorist by holding and choking his neck so that he would lose control of his own body, is a good example of the benefits of prior training. As we came to learn days after the incident, Stone was a trained medical technician and a member of the US Air Force while Skarlatos was a member of the National Guard. Their training may have helped them to recognize that the AK rifle had jammed. And it was at that moment they decided, "Let's get him now." Although Skarlatos later stated that his decision was driven by either instinct or "survival mode," I am inclined to attribute that instinct to prior skills obtained in the military. If it were me, for example, I probably would have just fallen to the ground and waited for the bullets to rain over me.

This rare show of bravery that prevented the massacre of passengers in the train earned the three men one of France's highest honors, awarded by President François Hollande on August 24, 2015. In a statement, President Hollande said: In the name of France, I would like to thank you. The whole world admires your bravery. It should be an example to all of us and inspire us. You put your lives at risk in order to defend freedom." He further added, "If the jihadist threat is to remain with us—and nothing suggests that it will stop—the behavior of individuals toward the imminence of violence could become a crucial factor. If more people are willing to risk their lives by standing up to fight, then that will shift the psychological battle in favor of our societies (*BBC News*, "France train ..." 2015).

In the above situation, the French president seems to be appealing to a similar exercise of humanitarian values: courage, willingness, moral and social obligation, and altruism. What is equally important here is the recognition of courage and willingness to intervene in such situations that are generally dependent on prior exposure, training, and competence.

Medical-Related Emergencies

Studies conducted by Axelsson (2001) and Tanigawa et al. (2011) further affirm that bystanders trained in cardiopulmonary resuscitation (CPR) are often willing and ready to respond to cardiac arrest incidents that occur within close range. The authors also observed that saving a cardiac arrest victim is largely dependent on appropriate intervention, where appropriate means having the requisite competence. Such competence, achieved mostly through training, will often influence a bystander's willingness and readiness to provide direct and correct intervention. Additionally, a trained bystander is emotionally better prepared to intervene, whereas those without relevant skill may be scared to do anything. This study concludes that trained bystanders can potentially double the chances of survival for cardiac arrest victims that occur out of hospital settings. One other important take on these findings is that citizens trained in CPR are not only more likely (or willing) to perform one but also indirectly encourage others to acquire similar skills.

Probably the most frequently experienced emergency that requires instant responders is road accidents. In my lifetime to date, I have witnessed more road accident emergencies than any other form of emergency. Those who live in Nepal, Peru, China, and Turkey might cite earthquakes and the magnitude of their effects on human lives as the most frequently experienced types of emergency. Those who live in geographically low-lying nations of Bangladesh, the Philippines, Indonesia, and other smaller islands will probably mention floods as the most experienced form of disaster in their lives. Despite all of these differences, I want to briefly discuss further road accidents because the global statistics of their frequency, their magnitude, and their impact on human lives, health, and the economy is startling.

Road traffic accidents, according to the World Health Organization and Indian Institute of Technology Delhi training manual compiled by Mohan et al. (2002), caused the death of 1.2 million people (p. 11). That amounts to an average of 3,242 killed daily on the world's roads. Between twenty and fifty million individuals were injured or disabled due to road collisions. To put it differently, road traffic injuries were responsible for 2.1 percent of all deaths and therefore ranked eleventh as the leading cause of death globally. What is interesting (or expected) is that 90 percent of traffic-related deaths occurred in middle and low-income countries where about 81 percent of world's population lives. Suffice it to say that over 50 percent of deaths globally occur among ages between fifteen and forty-four years (Mohan et al., p. 13). Of all the total fatalities, 73 percent are males. The source indicates that this is unusually high given the fact that these countries own only about 20 percent of all vehicles on the planet. Africa, for example, has the highest mortality rate (28.3 deaths per 100,000) as table 1 illustrates, followed by the Eastern Mediterranean region at 26.4 deaths.

Given the magnitude of road traffic deaths and related injuries, and also their frequency, it is no wonder bystanders often experience these incidents and often try to intervene and do whatever they can to save victims involved. Recall the case in Utah (referenced in chapter 2) in which a motorcycle collided with a car on the highway by Utah State University. The bike rider was trapped underneath the vehicle that was already burning. Ordinary citizens rushed to the scene, with some lifting the vehicle up and the others trying to pull the rider out. In this case, these were ordinary people without any form of prior training. There was no evidence of any additional injury due to their rescue; the victim's life was saved.

WHO Region	Low-Income and Middle-Income Countries	High-Income Countries
Africa Region	28.3	--
Region of the Americas	16.2	14.8
Southeast Asia Region	18.6`	--
European Region	17.4	11.0
Eastern Mediterranean Region	26.4	19.0
Western Pacific Region	18.5	12.0

Table 1a: Road traffic injury rates (per 100,000 population) in WHO regions, 2002. Source: Mohan et al. (2006). Road traffic injury prevention: Training Manual, WHO and Indian Institute of Technology Delhi, p. 11.

Further studies on bystander experiences during as well as after road accidents, however, show it is not always true that bystanders will respond to motor vehicle accidents. Their responses are on the average controlled by physical, emotional, cognitive, and situational factors (Hall, Wotton, and Hutton, 2013). The study also found that response behaviors to road accidents were influenced by the nature of the emergency and the perceived injury sustained by the victims. For example, in the bus accident cited in the preface that my wife and I witnessed, some bystanders stopped briefly to see what had happened and then drove off. Others, like us, decided to stop and identify those who were still alive to see what we could do. Also, whereas we felt morally obligated to assist, others did not. As others (Darley and Latané, 1970) have opined, assessment of the potential costs (to the victim and to the bystander) do affect the decision by the would-be helpers in such incidents. Hall et al. (2013) further suggest in their study that bystander perceptions (e.g., victim condition or whether or not first aid is required) partly explain whether or not to jump in to assist victims of a road accident.

A related factor is fear. Bystanders' readiness to help or not to help in road accident emergencies is also determined by fear of two things: liability and the possibility of worsening the victim's injuries. I am inclined to say that this is generally true in most advanced nations where a good number of the population has been made aware of when not to move a victim—say out of an automobile involved in an accident. But for the rest of the developing nations (at least in my place of birth, Kenya), I would argue fear of liability and the potential for further worsening a victim's condition are not matters of concern. For the most part, bystanders think first of what they need to do to save a life in emergencies. Usually, the first thing is to try to move to safety the victim from a car wreck or fire.

Another point by Hall et al. (2013) is that the possession of knowledge has something to do with whether a bystander will or will not intervene in a motor vehicle accident. Although bystanders were found to be less likely to provide first aid, especially when the injuries were viewed as worse, the findings referenced by Hall et al. show that prior first aid training increased from 16.4 percent (with no training) to 87 percent (after training). This empirical evidence strongly suggests that training is indeed critical for increasing the confidence and willingness of a bystander to provide assistance to those involved in life-threatening situations such as road accidents. The relationship to the victim is also a factor that can often influence a bystander's decision to assist a victim. Statistics on this are quite interesting. For example, 7 percent of those involved in a study expressed interest in performing CPR on strangers, while 13 percent said they would do so for relatives and friends (Hall et al., 2013). Performing CPR in our age of communicable diseases such as HIV can pose a challenge to potential first responders (bystanders). Therefore, even though time and again statistics show that CPR can quickly restore breathing and a pulse, fear and lack of knowledge can potentially reduce the willingness to intervene in emergency situations.

One important lesson from these studies is that training and prior knowledge are important predictors of the degree of bystanders' willingness to assist in emergency situations. At the same time, however, training alone does not tell all. Fear, relationship to the victim, and perceptions are also important determinants. Moreover, emotional, physical, and cognitive challenges can also determine bystanders' decision to intervene even though they may possess the most relevant skills and training.

Mine Incident—Copiapo, Chile

On August 5, 2010, a group of thirty-thirty miners were trapped approximately 2,300 feet (701 meters) below the surface of the earth in the San Jose Mine by a huge rock that caused a cascading effect, thereby closing the only entry and exit. The mine was located about twenty-eight miles (forty-five kilometers) from the town of Copiapo in northern Chile. We can only imagine that when the incident occurred, there was nothing bystanders could do except shout for help. This was such a large and complex incident that any ordinary bystander could not contemplate trying to intervene. Soon after the news reached the government, the Chilean Navy submarine experts and other rescue teams called for further assistance after assessing the complexity involved. One of the first organizations to be reached was National Aeronautics and Space Agency (NASA). After embarking on the rather arduous assessment, and subsequently joined by other experts from around the globe, there was a glimpse of hope when a small video camera was inserted down under that brought images of the miners still alive and well. This was after seventeen days. After sixty-nine days in the ground, the team of experts was able to bring each miner at a time through a shaft. The process of bringing all of the miners to the surface took almost twenty-two hours in total. This was all thanks to the wonders of technology and training.

Collapsed Cyclist Saved by Trainer Bystander

It was on April 23, 2015, in Hanover, in the US state of New Hampshire, when Weiping Liu noticed a group of people on the side of the road. He pulled over and noticed that a man had collapsed, but the group could not offer any help even though they appeared willing. Liu quickly concluded that the cyclist had probably suffered a heart attack. He then suggested to the group that they should perform CPR to the victim. One person in the group responded that none of them knew how to perform CPR. Liu, who had previous training, performed CPR while paramedics were still on their way. Doctors and the paramedics later acknowledged that the quick action by Liu saved the life of the victim, Doug Tifft, who had no detectable pulse before CPR was performed. His quick intervention made Tifft's recovery much easier (Cassidy, 2015).

Umpqua Community College Shooting

In the mass shooting that took place on October 1, 2015, at Oregon's Umpqua Community College, twenty-six-year-old Christopher Harper-Mercer shot ten people and injured nine others before killing himself. Chris Mintz demonstrated not only heroism but also proved how training can be helpful. When Chris, an army veteran, heard the gunshots next door, he tried to talk the gunman down. Although the gunman shot him seven times, many now believe that had Chris not talked to the gunman (thereby slowing down his killing spree), the casualties would have been much higher. The negotiation tactics employed by Chris have been employed in a number of cases, especially to talk potential suicide victims, for example, out of their intentions.

Trained Actor Assists 9/11 Firefighters

Soon after terrorist planes destroyed the World Trade Towers in New York on September 11, 2011, previously trained firefighter-turned Hollywood actor Steve Buscemi rapidly made his way to the incident site to assist other firefighters (Snopes.com). He and others dug and sifted through the heaps of rubble looking for survivors. His ability to provide support to the New York City Firefighters demonstrates the importance of training.

Emergency Training Initiatives

At the turn of this century, there has been an increased and concerted effort to provide ordinary citizens with the skills that they can use to save themselves and others from random life-threatening incidents. At the international level, the United Nations, through its platform for Space-Based Information for Disaster Management and Emergency Response (SPIDER), provides training on emergency preparedness and response to national governments in order to enhance citizen knowledge and the capacity to respond to disasters. Similar initiatives have been initiated at the international level across the globe.

One area in which public institutions, particularly schools, have taken a keen interest is the prevention of sexual assault. This is because in some cultures where males still have dominant roles, actions aimed at the prevention of sexual assault have been lukewarm at best. Moreover, policies to mitigate such offenses lack full-force implementation. Even where they are enforced, offenders at times go unpunished. This is the case in emerging democracies where ordinary citizens lack voice and systems are corrupt. The good thing is that bystander intervention training is increasingly taking root. This kind of training is offered ostensibly with skills to act safely and effectively in sexual assault cases. Training provides a menu of choices; for example, whether a person looking to intervene should use physical force, call for help, create a distraction, or seek intervention helpers.

Chapter 7

Recommendations

Despite attempts in the previous chapters to show the importance of recognizing the important role that bystanders play in many isolated cases of emergencies around the world, the following question ought to be asked before instituting policies or requirements for involvement bystanders: How can we use them more effectively in a way so as to not endanger their lives? The recommendations identified in this final chapter are premised on a conceptual change (or paradigm shift) in the way we deal with all life-threatening emergencies. It is one that proposes moving away from relying solely on the core group of professionals (EMS) to developing a culture of preparedness among all citizens. To do so, policymakers must make relevant laws that include willing citizens and volunteers to protect themselves, their family, and property instead of waiting for professional rescuers in all cases of emergency. Otherwise, nations generally enact laws to regulate disaster response activities. These laws quite often provide legal frameworks for disaster management. On the other hand, administrative agencies responsible for emergency management do not perform their mandated duties, but, in light of limited resources, they must try to reach out to ordinary citizens by providing them with training and then incorporate them into the planning and execution stages. Ordinary citizens and communities likewise must be reminded that they have a responsibility to know what to do in case of disasters and minor emergencies. This way, societies can become more resilient, and the loss of lives and property can be minimized.

Thus, given the evidence so far adduced, it seems reasonable to seriously consider what bystanders can do to save lives in emergencies that occur within their proximity. Whether it is a medically related emergency (suffocation or cardiac arrest), road accidents (getting passengers out from a burning car), drowning (rescuing incapacitated swimmer), house fires (removing an elderly person in a wheelchair), or simply calling for emergency services, bystanders can save lives through their actions. This final chapter presents recommendations to policy makers, government agencies, nonprofits, and individual citizens on how best to prepare for and respond to emergencies. More importantly is how these bodies can incorporate bystanders into emergency planning and to prepare them with lifesaving skills. This call is also based on the fact that state resources are often limited in their ability to address all emergencies that occur at every place in any community or city.

Here are some recommendations that various entities, as well as individual citizens, can do to engage bystanders and prepare them for unrelenting emergencies:

Policymakers

I start first with a caveat: In more developed societies such as the United States, Canada, Britain, France, Germany, Australia, and several European countries, the role of bystanders in emergency response is discouraged to a large extent. Policy makers don't want bystanders to have a formal role in emergency response. This is because they generally don't know what to do in disastrous emergencies; they can become victims in the process of helping or barriers to effective rescue by professionals. To institute policies that include bystanders is like government agencies abandoning their role. As James Keck, a professor of Homeland Security and Emergency Preparedness at Virginia Commonwealth University, puts it, "bystanders can be [more of a] burden than it is worth" (personal communication, October 12, 2015).

Despite this state of inertia among policymakers in the West, calls are being made for public officials to recognize the capabilities and motivation of bystanders in providing additional human capital (especially physical capital) freely and therefore to incorporate them into emergency response and preparedness. It is this recognition that triggered the signing into law by President George W. Bush the Post-Katrina Emergency Reform Act (PKEMRA) in 2006. The primary goal of that policy was to motivate ordinary citizens to get involved in community emergency response teams and also to assist professional rescuers to better save lives and property in a timely fashion. Countries such as Japan have enacted several laws (Disaster Relief Act, Fire Services Act, Disaster Countermeasures Basic Act, and River Act and Flood Control Act) to help prepare, mitigate, and respond to disasters. Elements of training are included.

Administrative Agencies

Agencies tasked with emergency response planning, preparedness, mitigation, and recovery have a lot on their plate, given limited resources, large populations, and the geographic spread in which citizens live. Therefore, whenever emergencies occur, these specialized agencies must respond no matter how long it takes them. As has been shown in the preceding chapters, many of these agencies often fail to arrive in a timely fashion; of course, there are exceptions. In many cities in the United States, including the ones I have personally witnessed, it takes an average five minutes for emergency services (EMS) to arrive at the scene of an emergency. I want to believe that this is also true for many European nations even though the average response time will be different in smaller and larger cities. Despite this degree of efficiency, many municipalities and other developing countries recognize the importance of engaging organized volunteers (with some prior training) and bystanders (with no training).

To effectively engage these nonprofessionals, it is recommended that these emergencies provide training to these groups of first responders. The training can focus on minor injuries, extraction of victims from collapsed buildings following events such as earthquakes or hurricanes, and performing basic first aid (such as attending to bleeding or performing CPR). FEMA, for example, has an ongoing online training program through the Emergency Management Institute; other national governmental agencies can borrow a leaf from their experience. EMI is the national body charged with the development and delivery of emergency management training. Hence the goal is to improve the capabilities of federal, state, and local government officials, private sectors, and the public in order to reduce the negative effects of major disasters and other forms of life-threatening emergencies. The curriculum includes sections such as: "Are You Ready: An in-depth guide to citizen preparedness and community preparedness." These sessions are available for free online. Another relevant agency is the National Training and Education Division (NTED). It provides training to traditional (professional) first responders so that they can be better prepared for all sorts of emergencies amid scarcity (https://training.fema.gov/).

A number of states have embarked on citizens' training (Citizens Corps) to better prepare them for emergencies and also to equip them with relevant skills to save themselves and others, as well as their property. For example, in 2014, Governor Andrew Cuomo launched a Citizen Preparedness Corps Training Program that was expected to train 100,000 New Yorkers on proper preparation for emergencies or disasters. The initiative aims to equip citizens with essential skills and resources to prepare for and recover from emergencies and disasters. The governor emphasized the importance of training citizens to better respond to emergencies either as part of organized groups or as family units. Similar programs as well as community emergency response teams (CERTS) (already launched in twenty-eight states) are part of the bigger effort to equip ordinary citizens, who by default are bystanders, with the requisite skills.

Public-Private Partnerships

Collaboration between the official emergency service agencies and the private sector is another means to effectively accomplish the ever-growing task of responding to the galloping rate of disasters. In the United States, public-private partnership in emergency management is nothing new. More recently, we have seen FEMA working closely with Wal-Mart and Target to provide needed supplies and storage facilities. This is also true with power (electricity) companies. When disasters occur, power companies must be part of the response team, as they know where power line are located; collaborative effort facilitates quick restoration of power.

After witnessing the chaos immediately after the bombing of US embassy in Nairobi in April 1998 (see chapter 2) and the extent to which the emergency systems were overwhelmed, I strongly believe that the more effective way to strengthening resiliency to disasters is to encourage partnerships with the private and nonprofit sectors. This builds on the idea of synergy; these other sectors often have the needed knowledge, skills, equipment, and other supplies that the public sector may not have. After the bombing, it was the ordinary citizens who provided the much-needed service of transporting the injured to hospitals. They did so by using their own vehicles and private taxis. And when the Somalia-based Al Shaabab terrorist group attacked shoppers at Westgate Mall in Nairobi (September, 2013), private citizens came in scores to complement the city's meager emergency transport services. It therefore seems reasonable to suggest that partnerships with private companies would yield a greater good for the society.

The main concern is, how are such partnerships to be facilitated? One approach is for relevant public agencies to provide some kind of incentives to willing companies. Another, although somewhat unpopular approach, is to compel government agencies to incorporate private sector and nonprofit agencies into emergency management—say in a particular city—including planning, preparedness, mitigation, response, and recovery. Nongovernmental bodies should be made to understand that they are part of the society and when an emergency strikes a city or municipality, they can be affected as well in many ways (e.g., disruption of water and power supply and injuries to some of their employees). The government therefore should desist emergency planning and management in isolation. All relevant sectors must be invited as part of the team.

Communities and Ordinary Citizens

There is no doubt that communities as social entities can make a difference in mitigating and responding to emergencies effectively. Whenever disasters occur or a fire erupts in a neighbor's house, people living in the vicinity will come out to assist, usually by calling for help.

There is a growing interest, as we have seen in at least twenty-eight US states, in community action to address black swan events whenever they occur. The fury of nature can incapacitate official local resources. This is why local communities can capitalize on their numbers and cohesion to respond.

This responsibility, however, does not just lie with organized community groups but also with ordinary citizens. We have the responsibility for our lives, that of the family, and to some extent our neighbors. Being responsible for your neighbor will depend on one's culture. In collective societies (such as Africa, Asia, Mexico, and the Caribbean, for example), being responsible for your neighbor's welfare is an expected practice of good behavior. However, in individualist societies, such as France, the United Kingdom, and the United States, individuals care for themselves and close members of the family (Geert Hostede. com). Although these two theoretical perspectives have been widely tested in a number of studies following Geert Hofstede's groundbreaking analyses of the characteristics of global cultures, my own observation is that extending help to a needy neighbor, especially in time of need and emergency, is just as common in Western societies as in Asia and Africa. My encounters with individual citizens in the Middle East, Africa, and Central Asia confirm this tendency: people are for people. The Arabs call it *elnasi le elnas*. People, regardless of their geographic locations, have the tendency to demonstrate empathy—which is a precursor to altruism. This statement does not imply universality, however. Among the human race, there are a number of individuals who disdain altruism and strongly believe that each person must fend for him or herself.

Despite these cultural nuances and the basic premises discussed by this book, it is recommended that ordinary citizens should by necessity acquire lifesaving skills such as performing CPR, preventing a child from choking, or even delivering babies—a task often deferred to professionals, and yet occasionally untrained bystanders are faced with these challenging tasks. Knowing how to deliver babies, at least for men, can be invaluable if your spouse's water breaks on the way to the hospital and it can't wait another five minutes. Being able to prevent bleeding from punctured skin and rescuing one from drowning are skills that anyone will be proud to possess. Hence, training is not only necessary for knowing how to assist the injured, but it can also equip us with determining when to seek help from experts.

Conclusion

I conclude this book by looking back at the realities on the streets, villages, open seas, and workplaces, where ordinary citizens are driven by their instincts (potent instinct) to assist those faced by life-threatening events. From China, Afghanistan, India, Syria, Kenya, the Gambia, Egypt, Ireland, Germany, Croatia, Hungary, Sweden, and the United States, humans seem to have this unifying characteristic—empathy and, by extension, altruism. These attributes are demonstrated by their unabated readiness to rescue those who face life-threatening situations, be it war, hunger, hurricane, or an attack by a lion. Some theorists have suggested that this helping behavior is part of our being human. It is also true of animals. We see time and again on television sets and YouTube videos how African buffalos, for example, form cohesive groups to attack lions that have either caught one of their calves or are about to launch an attack on one of their own.

The instinct to save one of your own species has been defended by some scholars by suggesting that we will do anything to protect human DNA from extinction. Does this explain why animals such as African buffalos will fight to protect a member of their own species from ferocious attack by a lion? If this is true, then it would make sense for us to always rescue others in danger and not kill our fellow human beings. This view seems to contradict the growing level of human insanity as demonstrated by senselessly killing members of our own species in the name of hatred, anger, greed, mental hallucinations, and limited resources and space. Some of us, however, believe that, despite our burgeoning population of 7.3 billion, we have plenty of space, food, water, and other desirable resources to survive on. I think at the core of this issue is a lack of fairness in the distribution and redistribution of available resources. Another source of the problem is human greed that is responsible for what appears to be artificial scarcity. Several published reports and documents have attempted to show that overall, there is enough food and other resources for all of us on the planet. The problem is misdistribution. Others privileged to have more simply do not have the right to hoard their wealth, be it food, water, or medicine.

In addition to greed, there is anger, a destructive attribute unique to humans. Extreme anger, if not controlled, can lead humans to make harmful and irrational decisions. Humans, as we know, are the only species that will kill members of their own species almost with passion. On the contrary, only a handful of animals do this to their own species. A lion, for example, possesses powerful paws and teeth, and yet when another lion crosses its territory, the invader will simply give up and run way once it notices it is not welcome. Of course, other animals will kill their own species for food but not because they are fighting for space or grass that might be limited. Rather, they are able to share amicably dwindling resources such as waters and available grass without denying the other member of the kingdom. So where does this leave us?

Despite our greed and anger and occasional outbursts aimed at dominating the weak, on a one-on-one basis we seem to be quite rational and considerate. That is why an American, for example, who is vacationing in the Russian beaches of Crimea will rescue a teenager from Moscow who is drowning. She will do this even if politically the two nations don't see eye-to-eye. Also, regardless of our admirable level of self-acclaimed rationality, we still cannot master the forces of nature. We watch with awe and disbelief at the invasion and destruction of property and of our lives by the forces of nature. We often try to predict, based on history, when the next earthquake is likely to occur so that we can prepare. But sadly, volcanoes erupt when we least expect them, with destructive effects so widespread we cannot rescue everyone before the volcano ejects venomous shreds of fire and plume. Moreover, whenever similar forces of nature occur—hurricanes, tornadoes, and floods—we, in turn, realize how important it is to better prepare so that loss of life and property is minimized. That is why training is an important element of emergency preparedness and mitigation.

Equally important is our ability to respond to these rare (black swan) events. As humans have discovered over several centuries, learning "how to" is the only recipe to progress and antidote to destruction exacted by forces of nature. It is also important to recognize that these antidotes—awareness, training, and collaboration—can significantly reduce both short- and long-term costs of any disaster. For example, human costs (or loss of lives) can be reduced if people know what to do in order to better prepare and respond to disasters common to their communities (e.g., hurricanes and tornadoes in the US Midwest states, wildfires in the west and mountain states, and avalanches in alpine territories). Similarly, costs such as loss and replacement of property, increased insurance, or loss of service associated with lack of awareness can be remedied by the acquisition of basic lifesaving skills. Whether at the individual or family level, actions to learn how to prevent or respond to emergencies can have cascading effects at the community level, thus making them more resilient to disasters.

Finally, as I have tried to justify in each chapter, bystanders can save lives before professionals arrive at the scene of an incident. They readily jump into action in the face of a life-threatening incident in order to save other humans. This is true particularly for easily discernable incidents and also when the costs of doing so are perceived to be relatively low. Of course we ought to be reminded that, whereas bystanders are driven by their natural instincts to assist those in danger, this instinct can occasionally be driven, determined, or even constrained by factors such as the presence of other witnesses (bystander effect), fear, and the relationship she or he might have with the victim. Although the bystander effect (i.e., the possibility that one's willing behavior to assist is constrained in the absence of many witnesses) has its merits, particularly in major cities where diffusion of responsibility tends to be the norm, the opposite is true with violent crimes. According to studies cited in earlier chapters, regardless of the presence of a large number of witnesses, our helping behavior will be demonstrated by trying to rescue the victim of such crimes. This is because the level of certainty in such incidents is higher, and the associated costs (to the helper and to the victim) are much easier to assess in a matter of minutes.

Bystander intervention in emergencies can be a cost-cutting measure for agencies involved in this essential role. Bystanders provide help willingly and for free. They do it out of natural instincts because, as the Arabs say, *"Elnasi le elnas"* ("People are for people"). Why then can't policy makers and emergency management agencies incorporate them into planning and execution? It seems reasonable to admit that bystander intervention in emergencies is simply "the right thing to do" as 71 percent of my 2012 survey participants confirmed.

Index

Appendices

Appendix 1

Checklist for Responding to Different Types of Emergencies

For hurricane emergency, visit: http://www.vaemergency.gov/.

For flood emergency, visit: http://www.redcross.org/.

For tsunami emergency, visit: http://www.redcross.org/.

For earthquake emergency, visit: http://www.redcross.org/.

For landslide emergency, visit: http://www.redcross.org/.

For volcanic eruption, visit: http://www.redcross.org/.

For wildfire emergency, visit: http://www.redcross.org/.

For tornado emergency, visit: http://www.redcross.org/.

For drought emergency, visit: www.fema.gov *or* www.ready.gov.

For outdoor water conservation tips, visit: www.fema.gov *or* www.ready.gov.

For pandemic emergency, visit: www.fema.gov *or* www.ready.gov.

For terrorism emergency, visit: www.fema.gov *or* www.ready.gov.

For nuclear blast emergency, visit: www.fema.gov *or* www.ready.gov.

For cyber attack preparedness, visit: www.fema.gov *or* www.ready.gov.

For chemical emergency, visit: www.fema.gov *or* www.ready.gov.

For sinkhole emergency, visit: http://disaster.ifas.ufl.edu/PDFS/CHAP18/D18-05.PDF.

For home fire emergency, visit: http://www.redcross.org/.

For automobile accident preparedness in underdeveloped nations, visit: http://www.who.int/en/.

For electrocution emergency, visit: http://www.safetyservicescompany.com/topic/training/electrocution-rescue-should-never-add-another-victim/.

For starting, implementing and maintaining community emergency response team (CERT), visit: https://www.fema.gov/about-community-emergency-response-team.

Bibliography

Chapter 1

Axelsson, A. "Bystander cardiopulmonary resuscitation: Would they do it again?" *Cardiovasc Nurs* 16, vol. 1 (2001): 15–20.

Eberhard, M. J. W. "The evolution of social behavior by kin selection." *Quarterly Review of Biology* 50 (1975): 1–33.

Forrert, T, R. "Group emergence in disasters." In *Disasters: Theory and Research*, edited by E. L. Quarantelli, 106–125. Beverly Hills, CA: Sage, 1978.

"Good Samaritans." Definitions. U.S. Legal.com.

Hoffman, M. L. "Is altruism part of human nature?" *Journal of Personality and Social Psychology* 40, vol. 1 (1981): 121–137.

Latane, B. and Darley, J.M. *Help in a Crisis: Bystander Response to an Emergency.* Morristown, NJ: General Learning Press, 1970.

Luke 10:25–37. BibleGateway.com.

McDonald, P. Charlesworth, S., & Graham, T. (2015). Action or inaction: Bystander intervention in workplace sexual harassment. *International Journal of Human Resource Management*, 1–19.

Quarantelli, E.L. (Ed.). (1978). *Disasters: Theory and research*. Beverly Hills, CA: Sage.

Schwartz, S. H and Gottlieb, A. (1980). Bystander anonymity and reactions to emergencies. *Journal of Personality and Social Psychology, 39*(3), 418–430.

Solnit, R. (2009). *A paradise built in hell: The extraordinary communities that arise in disasters (1ˢᵗ Edition)*. London: Penguin Books.

Staub, E. (1978). *Positive social behavior and morality: Social and Personal Influence, Vol. 1*. Academic Press: New York.

Staub, E. (1989). The evolution of bystanders, German psychoanalysis, and lessons for today. *Political Psychology, 10*(1), 39–52.

Wakefield, J. C. (1993). Is altruism part of human nature? Toward a theoretical foundation for the helping professions. *Social Service Review, 67*(3), 406–458.

Chapter 2

Becker, E. (1972). From animal to human reactivity. In *Human nature: Theories, conjecture, and descriptions* (198–205). Metuchen, NJ.

From, E. (1972). Man—Wolf or Sheep? In *Human nature: Theories, conjecture, and descriptions* (109–120). Metuchen, NJ.

Greenfeld, L. (n. d.). Are human emotions universal? *Psychology Today*. Retrieved from www.psychologytoday.com

Hawley, P. H. (2014). The duality of human nature: Coercion and prosociality in youths' hierarchy ascension and social success. *Current Directions in Psychological Science, 23*(6), 433–438.

Michel, J.J. (1972). The many possibilities for human behavior. In *Human nature: Theories, conjecture, and descriptions* (67–77). Metuchen, NJ.

Midgley, M. (1995). *Beast and Man: The roots of human nature*. London and New York: Routledge.

Murphy, G. (1972). Three kinds of human nature. In *Human nature: Theories, conjecture, and descriptions* (78–94). Metuchen, NJ.

Pojman, L. P. (2006). *Who are we? Theories of human nature*. New York and Oxford: Oxford University Press.

Sigel, A. and Victoroff, J. (2009). Understanding human aggression: New insights from neuroscience. *International Journal of Law and Psychiatry*, 32, 209–215.

Wilson, J.R.S. (1972). *Emotion and object*. Cambridge: Cambridge at the University Press.

Chapter 3

(2003 February 21). At least 96 killed in nightclub inferno. CNN News. Retrieved from http://www.cnn.com.

(2012, December 14). Sandy Hook shooting: What happened? CNN News. Retrieved from http://www.cnn.com.

(2012, November, 4). The most incredible Hurricane Sandy survival story. NBC News. Retrieved from http://www.nbcnewyork.com.

(2013, Sept, 2). Swissair Flight 111 tragedy still raw 15 years later. CBC News. Retrieved from http://www.cbc.ca.

(2014 April 28). South Korea ferry disaster: Footage shows crew being rescued. The Guardian. Retrieved from http://www.theguardian.com.

(2015, May 13). Amtrak train crash survivors describe chaos. CBS News. Retrieved from http://www.cbsnews.com.

Barker, A. (2014, November 22). Volunteers save lives in Vientiane, Laos, where road is among world's worst. *ABC News*. Retrieved from http://www.abcnews.com

Charlton, C. (2015, June 28). You must kill us first, but we're are Muslim: Tourist reveal how hotel workers formed 'human shield' to stop gun maniac shooting more dead as Britons tell how they played dead to survive. Daily Mail. Retrieved from http://www.dailymail.co.uk.

Darley, J.M. & Latane, B. (1968). Bystander intervention in emergencies: Diffusion of responsibility. *Journal of Personnel and Social Psychology, 8*, 377–383.

Fischhoff, B. (2005, August 7). A Hero in Every Aisle Seat. The New York Times. Retrieved from http://www.nytimes.com.

Hoffman, M. L. (1981). Is altruism part of human nature? *Journal of Personality and Social Psychology, 40*(1), 121–137.

Hutchins, B & Emert, H. (2013, January 27). Horror in Brazil: Fire kills 232, hundreds more injured in blaze. New York Daily News. Retrieved from http://www.nydailynews.com.

Ikowitz, C. (2015, November 13). The fearless father who threw himself on a suicide member, saving 'hundreds' of lives in Beirut. The Washington Post. Retrieved from http://www.washingtonpost.com.

Latane, B. & Darley, J. M. (1968). *Group inhibition of bystander intervention in emergencies. Journal of Personality and Social Psychology, 10*(3), 215–221.

Llyod, B. (2015, May 18). Couple rescued from burning car in North Carolina. KRIS 6 News. Retrieved from http://www.kristv.com.

Herman, R. (2011, May 12). In disasters, first responders are us. Yahoo Contributor Network. Retrieved from http://www.yahoo.com.

Harlan, C. (2014, April 27). After ferry disaster, a Katrina-lie reckoning in South Korea. The Washington Post. Retrieved from http://www.washingtonpost.com.

Jones, E. (2013, October 29). Police suspects in Tiananmen car crash. The Guardian. Retrieved from http://www.theguardian.com.

Petal, M. A., Celep, U., Tuzun, C., & Green, R. (2004). Teaching structural hazards awareness for preparedness and community response. *Bulletin of Earthquake Engineering, 2,* 155– 171.

PeopleOfAR. (2014, February 8). True Story of a real life superhero: Shavarsh Karapetyan.
Retrieved from: http://www.peopleofar.com/2014/02/08/true-story-of-a-real-life-superhero-shavarsh-karapetyan/

McDonald, P. Charlesworth, S., and Graham, T. (2015). Action or inaction: Bystander intervention in workplace sexual harassment. *International Journal of Human Resource Management,* 1–19.

Shasta, Darlington, (2013, January 29). Brazil club survivor remembers the man who saved her life. CNN News. Retrieved from http://www.cnn.com.

Snopes.Com. (2011). Steve Buscemi. http://www.snopes.com/rumors/buscemi.asp. Retrieved from http://www.nytimes.com

Schwirtz, M. (2013, January 27). Fire at a Nightclub in Southern Brazil. The New York Times. Retrieved from http://www.nytimes.com.

Holy Bible International Version. (1984). "Voice Heard in Ramah," Mathew, Chapter 2, Verse 18.

Winter, M. (2012, December 14). Tales of Sandy Hook heroism, young and old. USA Today. Retrieved from http://www.usatoday.com.

Chapter 4

Frey, B.S., Savage, D. A., and Torgler, B. (2010). Interaction of natural survival instincts and internalized social norms exploring the Titanic and Lusitania disasters. *Proc Natl Acad Sci* USA, 107 (11), 4862–4865.

Garber, J. (1997). Beyond dualism – the social construction of nature and the natural and social construction of human beings. *Progress in Human History*, 21(1), 1–17.

Popper, K. and Eccles, J.C. (1997). The self and its brain. Berlin: Springer-Verlag.

Chapter 5

Barman, M. (2015, July 9). South Carolina governor signs bill removing Confederate flag from statehouse grounds. The Washington Post. Retrieved from http://www.washingtonpost.com.

Borden, J. & Berman, M. (2015, June 23). South Carolina lawmakers discuss moving Confederate flag, while Amazon and Walmart join the debate. The Washington Post. Retrieved from http://www.washingtonpost.com.

Bradner, E. (2015, June 30). Confederate flag debate: A state-by-state round up. CNN Politics. Retrieved from http://www.cnn.com.

Browning, J. B. (n. d.). Union Carbide: Disaster at Bhopal. Union Carbide Corporation.

Enders, J. (2010). The 'miracle babies' of Mexico City: 25 years later. GlobalPost. Retrieved from http://www.globalpost.com.

FEMA. About Community Emergency Response Teams. Retrieved July 14, 2015, from http://www.fema.gov.

Georges, L. C., Winer, R. L., & Keller, S. R. (2013). The angry juror: Sentencing decisions in First-Degree murder. *Applied Cognitive Psychology, 27,* 156–166.

HistoryNet.com. The Civil War. Retrieved June 30, 2015 from histroynet. com/civilwar.

Homeland Security. (2002). Homeland Security Act of 2002. Retrieved October 30, 2015 from http://www.dhs.gov/ homeland-security-act-2002.

Ingraham, C. (2015, June 21). How the Confederacy lives on in the flags of seven southern states. The Washington Post. Retrieved from http://www.washingtonpost.com.

Kane, P. & Phillip, A. (2015, July 9). As S. C. prepares to lower battle flag, Boehner calls for Confederate review. The Washington Post. Retrieved from http://www.thewashingtonpost.com.

Learner, J.S. & Keltner, D. (2000). Beyond valence: Toward a model of emotion-specific influences on judgement and choice. *Cognition and Emotion, 14,* 473–493.

Library of Congress. (2015). Bill Summary & Status, 109th Congress (2005–2006) S.2271 CRS Summary. Retrieved from http://thomas.loc.gov/ cgi- in/bdquery/z?d109:SN02271:@@@D&summ2=m&hhttp:// thomas.loc.gov/

Mankad, A. (2012). Decentralized water systems: Emotional influences on resource decision making. *Environmental International, 44,* 128–140.

Barbara, M. & Martin, J. (2015, June 28). 5 days that left a Confederate flag wavering and likely to fall. The New York Times. Retrieved from http://www.nytimes.com.

U.N. Org. (2015). General Assembly-Quick Links. Retrieved on October 30, 2015 from http://research.un.org/en/docs/ga/quick/regular/20.

Payne, Ed, & Ford, D. (2015, July 15). South Carolina bill to remove Confederate flag moves to House. CNN Politics. Retrieved from http://www.cnn.com.

Plumer, B. (2013 April 11). Gun experts grade the Manchin-Toomey bill: A step forward, but a small step. The Washington Post. Retrieved from http://www.washingtonpost.com.

Sadler, M. S., Lineberger, M., Correll, J., & Park, B. (2005). Emotions, attributions, and policy endorsement in response to the September 11th terrorist attacks. *Basic and Applied Social Psychology, 27*(3), 249–258.

Self, J. (2015, July 8). Governor Haley to hold bill signing ceremony Thursday afternoon. The Buzz. Retrieved from http://www.thestate.com.

Small, D. A. & Lerner, J. S. (2008). Emotional policy: Personal sadness and anger shape judgments about a welfare case. *Political Psychology, 29*(2), 149–168.

Shear, M.D. (2015, June 22). Making a point, Obama invokes a painful slur. The New York Times. Retrieved from http://www.nytimes.com.

The 9/11 Commission Report: Final Report of the National Commission on terrorist attacks upon the United States. 9/11 Report.

Time Staff. (2013, April 17). President Obama's speech on gun control bill defeat (Transcript). TIME. Retrieved from http://www.time.com.

The United Nations Office for Disaster Risk Reduction. Retrieved from http://www.UNISDR.org.

Chapter 6

(2015, August 25). France train shooting: Hollande awards Legion d'honneur. BBC News. Retrieved from http://www.bbc.com. Related article: "France train shooting: Hollande thanks 'heroes' who foiled gunman."

Acemoglue. D. & Robinson, J. A. (2012). *Why nations fail: The origins of power, prosperity, and poverty*. New York: Crown Business.

Axelsson, A. (2001). Bystander cardiopulmonary resuscitation: Would they do it again? *J Cardiovasc Nurs, 16*(1), 15–20.

Basic Concepts. (2010). *Chapter 1: Basic concepts in cross-training*. Taylor and Francis Group, LLC.

Curry. G. D. (2011). Synergistic protection: The roadmap for improving citizen disaster preparedness response. *Society and Business Revie, 6*(2), 121–130.

Cassidy, M. (2015, June 22). Quick action by bystanders help save heart attack victim. Valley News. Retrieved from http://www.vnews.com.

Federal Emergency Management Agency. Community Emergency Response Teams. Retrieved September 22, 2015 from http://www.fema.gov/community-emergency-response-teams.

Frahm, K.A., Garden, P.J., Brown, L. M., Rogoff, D.P., and Troutman, A. (2014). Community- based disaster coalition training. *Journal of Public Health Management Practice, 20*(5), 111–117.

Geigher, B. F., Firsing III, S. L., Beric, B. & Rodgers, J. B. (2013). Readying the health education specialist for emergencies. *American Journal of Health Education, 44*, 128– 133.

Hall, A., Wotton, K., & Hutton, A. (2013). Bystander experiences at and after a motor vehicle accident: A review of the literature. *Australian Journal of Paramedicine, 10*(4), 1–11.

Kim, H. (2014). Learning from UK disaster exercises: policy implications for effective emergency preparedness. *Disasters, 28*(4), 846–857.

Peate, W. F. & Mullins, J. (2008). Disaster preparedness training for tribal leaders. *Journal of Occupational Medicine and Toxicology, 3*(2), 1–7.

Perry, R. W. (2004 June). Disaster exercise outcomes for professional emergency personnel and citizen volunteers. *Journal of Contingencies and crisis management, 12*(2), 64–75.

Tanigawa, K., Iwami, T., Nishiyama, C., Nonogi, H. & Kawamura, T. (2011). Are trained individuals more likely to perform bystander CPR? An observational study. *Resuscitation, 82*(1), 523–528.

Chapter 7
(No references listed)

www.ingramcontent.com/pod-product-compliance
Lightning Source LLC
Chambersburg PA
CBHW020520290526
45786CB00002B/689